高等职业院校电子信息类规划教材

电子信息专业英语

主　编　杨官霞　张晓燕　陈婷婷
副主编　侯卫东　胡　军　卫　祥
参　编　李　铭　廖智蓉　李文武

北京邮电大学出版社
www.buptpress.com

内 容 简 介

本书立足于学生,是一本与其他专业外语教材截然不同的教材,帮助学生解决在学习C语言(包括参加ACM竞赛)、软件安装、虚拟机、Linux系统,以及在汽车专业、城轨专业和电子信息专业的学习过程中碰到的相关英文问题,适合作为汽车专业、轨道交通专业、电子信息专业、计算机专业、软件专业、汽车电子专业、工业机器人专业等电子及计算机类专业教材,也可作为教师的参考书。

图书在版编目(CIP)数据

电子信息专业英语 / 杨官霞,张晓燕,陈婷婷主编. -- 北京:北京邮电大学出版社,2021.1(2021.7重印)
ISBN 978-7-5635-6326-5

Ⅰ. ①电… Ⅱ. ①杨… ②张… ③陈… Ⅲ. ①电子信息—英语 Ⅳ. ①G203

中国版本图书馆CIP数据核字(2021)第020606号

策划编辑:彭 楠　　责任编辑:王晓丹　左佳灵　　封面设计:七星博纳

出版发行:北京邮电大学出版社
社　　　址:北京市海淀区西土城路10号
邮政编码:100876
发 行 部:电话:010-62282185　传真:010-62283578
E-mail:publish@bupt.edu.cn
经　　　销:各地新华书店
印　　　刷:唐山玺诚印务有限公司
开　　　本:787 mm×1 092 mm　1/16
印　　　张:9.75
字　　　数:238千字
版　　　次:2021年1月第1版
印　　　次:2021年7月第2次印刷

ISBN 978-7-5635-6326-5　　　　　　　　　　　　　　　　　　定价:28.00元

・如有印装质量问题,请与北京邮电大学出版社发行部联系・

前　　言

编者在教学中,发现了学生有一些关于专业英语方面的问题。

一是有很多学生无法及时解决在 C 语言、Linux 系统、虚拟机等的学习中碰到的专业英语问题,要解决这些问题光看懂英文是不够的,还必须具备一定的专业知识才行。

二是汽车专业学生或轨道交通专业学生或电子信息专业学生所学习的专业英语教材过于专业,知识量太多,且不够实用,比如汽车类的专业英语书,学生学完之后连某些普通车辆如卡车、房车的英文名都说不上来。

三是大学生程序设计大赛中要使用一些英文,很多同学因为看不懂而与奖杯失之交臂。

为解决这些问题,本书立足于学生,是一本与其他专业外语教材截然不同的教材,既可以帮助学生解决学习 C 语言、软件安装、虚拟机、Linux 系统过程中碰到的问题,又可以解决电子信息专业、汽车专业和城轨专业学生在学习、工作和实习中碰到的相关英文问题。本书适合作为汽车专业、轨道交通专业、电子信息专业、计算机专业、软件专业、汽车电子专业等电子及计算机类专业教材,同时,也可作为教师的参考书。

第 1 章 C 语言专业英语,主要介绍了学生在使用 C 语言时在安装、调试、运行、编译等过程中所碰到的英文问题及解析和解决办法。

第 2 章汽车专业英语,主要介绍了汽车的车型、品牌、类别以及相关部件及其功能,尤其详细地介绍了发动机的工作过程,其中汽车品牌部分内容诙谐幽默,可读性很强。

第 3 章电子信息专业英语,主要介绍了专业词汇和一些电子信息专业英语的语法规则,有很强的指导性。

第 4 章城轨专业英语,主要解决城轨专业学生以后在实习和工作中所碰到的英文问题,诸如问路指路、售票退票、安全运营、行调指挥等。

第 5 章涉及其他专业英语,如 Linux 专业英语,该部分将该课程中学生可能会碰到的英文问题一网打尽。又如虚拟机专业英语,该部分主要介绍了安装虚拟机软件时学生经常会碰到的英文问题及解析。

第 6 章是计算机专业英语，主要是关于计算机专业英语中所碰到的一些语法、词汇和基本知识点。

附录是 ACM 比赛的相关专业英语词汇。

本书在编写过程中，结合了听力训练，相应的音频文件请从 http://www.buptpress.com 下载。

目 录

第1章 C语言常见错误罗列及解决办法 1
1.1 语法错误 1
1.2 软件安装设置错误 13

第2章 汽车专业英语 17
2.1 汽车简介 17
2.1.1 你能说出多少种车的英文名字？ 17
2.1.2 各种汽车 27
2.1.3 安全带 32
2.2 汽车标志 33
2.2.1 今日最受欢迎的汽车品牌 33
2.2.2 你认识这些汽车品牌吗？ 33
2.2.3 汽车制造商徽标 38
2.2.4 车标轶事 40
2.3 汽车基础知识 46
2.3.1 汽车的主要零件是什么？ 46
2.3.2 汽车发动机 49
2.3.3 引擎构造 50
2.4 保养 59
2.4.1 保养的类型和周期 59
2.4.2 车辆保养中的诊断 60
2.4.3 调回汽车里程表数值 61
2.5 汽车市场 62
2.5.1 怎样变成一个好的汽车销售？ 62
2.5.2 对话练习 63

第3章 电子信息专业英语 ·· 64

3.1 电子信息专业英语基础知识 ·· 64
3.2 翻译准则 ·· 70
3.3 电子信息专业英语阅读材料 ·· 71

第4章 城市轨道交通专业英语 ·· 76

4.1 问路和指路 ··· 76
4.1.1 常用问路指路的句式 ··· 76
4.1.2 各种问路指路情景对话 ·· 77
4.2 买票 ·· 80
4.2.1 买票充值情景对话 ·· 80
4.2.2 换卡退卡情景对话 ·· 85
4.3 提供信息和帮助 ··· 86
4.3.1 机器故障情景对话 ·· 86
4.3.2 其他帮助 ·· 89
4.4 安全工作 ·· 95
4.4.1 安全标志和指示 ··· 95
4.4.2 情景对话 ·· 98
4.5 行车组织原则 ·· 104
4.5.1 行车组织原则 ·· 104
4.5.2 行车指挥 ·· 105
4.5.3 正线信号控制 ·· 108

第5章 其他专业英语 ··· 112

5.1 系统中英文提示及解析 ·· 112
5.2 虚拟机英文提示及解决方法 ·· 119

第6章 计算机专业英语 ·· 122

6.1 计算机专业英语基础知识 ··· 122
6.1.1 用词的特点 ··· 122
6.1.2 语法的特点 ··· 122

6.1.3 句型结构 ·· 123
　　6.1.4 词汇类型 ·· 124
　　6.1.5 词汇来源 ·· 124
　　6.1.6 计算机专用术语与命令 ·· 128
　　6.1.7 网络专用术语 ··· 128
　6.2 计算机专业英语阅读 ·· 129
　　6.2.1 计算机的历史 ··· 129
　　6.2.2 计算机如何工作 ·· 130
　　6.2.3 关键词 ·· 133

参考文献 ·· 134

附录　ACM 词汇 ··· 135

第1章 C语言常见错误罗列及解决办法

1.1 语法错误

Figure 1-1　Parse error 1

源程序如下：
```
#include <stdio.h>
void main()
{  char a[]="a2汉字";
   int mm,i;
   /******** 1 *******/
   printf("请输入密码:");
   /******** 2 *******/
   scanf("%d",&mm);
```

```
    for(i=0;a[i]!='\0';i++)  /*各字符与mm作一次按位异或*/
        a[i]=a[i]^mm;
    puts(a);
    /*** 各字符与mm再作一次按位异或 ***/
    /******** 3 ********/
    for(i=0;a[i]!='\0';i++)
/****** 4 ******/
        a[i]=a[i]^mm;
    puts(a);
}
```

如 Figure 1-1 所示,错误提示 1:[error]D:\ccx\gc14.cpp:6:parse error before character 0241。

解析:错误在 D 盘 ccx 文件夹中 gc14.cpp 的 C 程序的第 14 行中,parse 表示从语法(句法)上分析有错误,错误地点在字符 0241 以前。这里的错误非常明显,即 printf 中用的是中文双引号,这是不符合语法规范的。

改正:将 printf("请输入密码:"),改为 printf("请输入密码:")即可。

Figure 1-2　Parse error 2

源程序如下：
```c
#include <stdio.h>
void main()
{ int a,n,i; long s = 0,t;
  /******* 1 ********/
  scanf("%d%d",&a,&n);
  /******* 2 ********/
  t = 0;
  /******* 3 **********/
  for(i = 1;i<= n;i ++){
    t = t * 10 + a;
    /******* 4 ********/
    s = t + s;
  }
  printf("%ld\n",s);
}
```

如 Figure 1-2 所示，错误提示 1：[error]D:\ccx\gc9.cpp:7:parse error before character 0241。

解析：错误在 D 盘 ccx 文件夹中 gc9.cpp 的 C 程序的第 7 行，parse 表示从语法(句法)上分析。有错误,错误地点在字符 0241 以前。这里的错误非常隐蔽，"t = 0;"这语句后面有看不见的隐含的格式字符——全角空格,当按住鼠标左键拖动时，就能发现有五个空格,同样地,12 行后面也有。

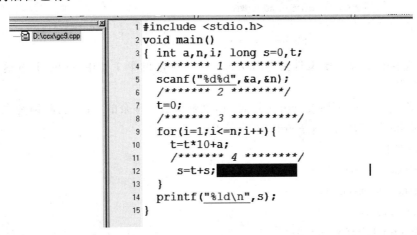

Figure 1-3 Hiding spaces

改正：将第 7 行后面以及第 12 行前后隐藏的全角空格(小方格)删掉就可以了。

源代码如下：
#include <stdio.h.h>
#include <math.h>

```
#define f(x) x*x-5.5*x+sin(x)
void main()
{   float x,max;
    max = f(0.0);
    for(x = 0.5;x <= 10;x = x + 0.5)
      if(f(x)>max) max = f(x);
    printf("%f\n",max);
}
```

如 Figure 1-4 所示,错误提示 1:[error]D:\ccx\tk6.cpp:1:stdio.h.h:No such file or directory。

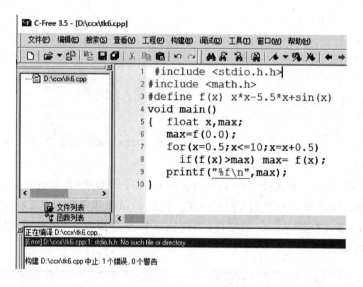

Figure 1-4　No such file or directory 1

解析:错误在 D 盘 ccx 文件夹中 tk6.cpp 的 C 程序的第 1 行中,stdio.h.h 这个文件或文件夹不存在。

改正:将"stdio.h.h"改为"stdio.h"即可,就是将最后多余的".h"去掉,因为在库文件中存在的是 stdio.h 文件,而不是 stdio.h.h 文件。

源代码如下:
```
#include <stdio.h>
#include <math.h>
long f(long n)
{   long m = fabs(n),y = 0;
    while(m>0) {
      y = y*10 + m%10; m = m/10;
    }
    return n<0? -y:y;
}
```

```
void main()
{
    printf("%ld\t",f(12345));
    printf("%ld\n",f(-34567));
}
```

如 Figure 1-5 所示,错误提示 1:[error]D:\ccx\tk8.cpp:2: math.h:No such file or directory。

Figure 1-5 No such file or directory 2

解析:错误在 D 盘 ccx 文件夹中 tk8.cpp 的 C 程序的第 2 行中,math.h 这个文件或文件夹不存在。

改正:将"math.h"前面多余的空格去掉即可,因为在库文件中存在的是 math.h 文件,而不是(空格)+math.h 文件。

还是上面这个程序,去掉前面的空格后,继续运行,出现如 Figure 1-6 所示的警告信息:

警告 1:D:\ccx\tk8.cpp:4:warning initialization to 'long int' from 'double'

解析:警告在 D 盘 ccx 文件夹中的 tk8.cpp 的 C 程序的第 4 行中,从 double 初始化为 long int。

处理方法:可忽略,因为一般是将 long int 转化为高级的 double,这里是将默认的 double 类型给 long int,特此警告,因为这里存储空间够用,所以不会影响程序运行,程序能正常执行,可忽略该警告。

Figure 1-6　Type mismatch

源程序如下：

```
#include <stdio.h>
void main()
{   char s[81]; int i;
    gets(s);
    for(i=0;s[i]!='\0';i++) {
        if(isupper(s[i]))
            s[i]=s[i]+32;
        else
            if(islower(s[i]))
                s[i]=s[i]-32;
        if(s[i]=='') s[i]='_';
    }
    puts(s);
}
```

如Figure 1-7所示，错误提示1：[error]D:\ccx\tk14.cpp:6:implict declaration of function ' int isupper(…)'。

解析：错误在D盘ccx文件夹中tk14.cpp的C程序的第6行中，函数"isupper(…)"的隐式声明有问题。

改正：问题在于要使用isupper(…)这个函数却没有定义，所以只要在第2行加上 #include <ctype.h>即可，在ctype.h这个头文件中存在关于函数isupper(…)的定义。

第1章　C语言常见错误罗列及解决办法

Figure 1-7　Implicit declaration of function

错误提示2：[error]D:\ccx\tk14.cpp:9:implict declaration of function 'int islower(...)'。

解析：错误在D盘ccx文件夹中tk14.cpp的C程序的第9行中，函数"islower(...)"的隐式声明有问题。

改正：方法和上面一样，上面加过了此处就不用再加了，因为islower(...)这个函数的定义也在ctype.h这个头文件里。

为方便大家调试，源代码如下：
＃include＜stdio.h＞
int f1()
{　　return 0x0b　&3；
}
char f2(int i)
{　char ch = 'a'；
    switch(i){
        case 1：
        case 2：
        case 3：ch ++ ；}
    return ch；
}
int f3(int x)

7

```
{   int s;
    if(x<0) s = -1;
    else if(x = 0) s = 0;
    else s = 1;
    return S;
}
main()
{   printf("%d\n",EOF);
    printf("%x\n",f1());
    printf("%c %c\n",f2(2),f2(5));
    printf("%d %d %d\n",f3(-1),f3(0),f3(10));
}
```

如 Figure 1-8 所示,错误提示 1:[error]D:\ccx\15cb3.cpp:3:'0xob' undeclared [first use this function]。

Figure 1-8 Undeclared data

解析:错误在 D 盘 ccx 文件夹中 15cb3.cpp 的 C 程序的第 3 行中,0xob 在初次使用时没有定义。

改正:将"0xob"改为"0x0b"即可,0x0b 是 ASCII 码的 11,或控制符垂直换行符。

错误提示 2:[error]D:\ccx\15cb3.cpp:10:parse error before charcter 0243。

解析:错误在 D 盘 ccx 文件夹中 15cb3.cpp 的 C 程序中的第 10 行中,parse 表示从语法(句法)上分析有错误,错误地点在字符 0243 以前。这时要检查程序中是不是含有非法字符,例如,应用英文符号的地方用了中文全角符号、中文空白符号,或错用了{}、()、""等。

改正:你如果仔细看,会发觉第十行中的冒号颜色和上两行不一样,这是因为它是全角中文符号的原因,改为半角的英文冒号即可。

错误提示 3:[error]D:\ccx\15cb3.cpp:18:Sundeclared [first use this function]。

解析:错误在 D 盘 ccx 文件夹中 15cb3.cpp 的 C 程序的第 18 行中,S 在初次使用时没有定义。

改正:将 S 改为 s,因为前面定义的一直是小写的 s,不是大写的 S,在 C 语言中大小写是不一样的变量名。

源程序如下:

```
# include <stdio.h>
double fun(float x)
{
return (x*x-6.5x+2);
}
main()
{
  float x;
  printf("   X     Y   \n");
for(x=-3;x<=3;x+=0.5)
 printf(" %.2f    %.2f\n",x,fun(x));
}
```

如 Figure 1-9 所示,错误提示 1:[error]D:\ccx\15cb8.cpp:4:nondigits in number and not hexadecimal。

Figure 1-9   Incorrect Chinese symbols

解析:错误在 D 盘 ccx 文件夹中 15cb8.cpp 的 C 程序的第 4 行中,有个数既不是数字也不是十六进制数。

改正:在 6.5 和 x 之间加个符号,如乘号"*"即可。

修改好之后,看看还有没有问题。

提示:注意第 9 行和第 11 行的双引号是不是英文半角形式。

源程序如下:

```c
#include <stdio.h>
void main()
{ /******** 1 *******/
    char a[7]='a2汉字';
    int i,j,k;
    /******** 2 *******/
    for(i=0;a[i]!='\0';i++){
        printf("a[%d]的机内码为:",i);
        for(j=1;j<=8;j++){
            k=a[i]&0x80;
            if(k!=0) putchar('1');
            /****** 3 *****/
            else putchar('0');
            /****** 4 *****/
            a[i]=a[i]<<1;
        }
        printf("\n");
    }
}
```

如 Figure 1-10 所示,错误提示 1:[error]D:\ccx\gc8.cpp:4:character contant too long。

Figure 1-10　Character constant is too long

10

解析：错误在 D 盘 ccx 文件夹中 gc8.cpp 的 C 程序的第 4 行中，字符常量太长。实际上就是字符数组应该用字符串而不是单个的字符常量，用单引号的是字符常量，字符串要用双引号。

改正：将第 4 行的那对单引号改为双引号即可。

错误提示 2：[error]D:\ccx\gc8.cpp:4:invalid initializer.

解析：错误在 D 盘 ccx 文件夹中 gc8.cpp 的 C 程序的第 4 行中，有无效的初始值设定项。问题是因为想把单引号引起的字符赋给字符数组。

改正：方法一样，将第 4 行的那对单引号改为双引号即可。

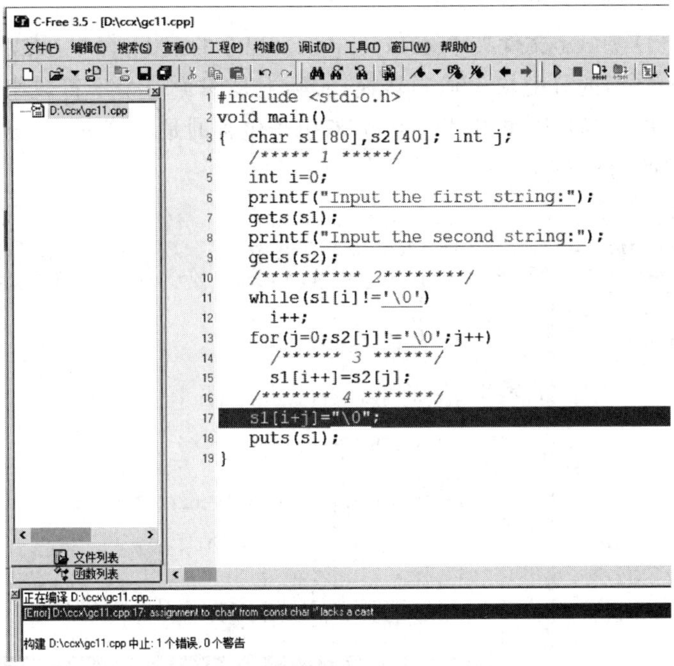

Figure 1-11　Type mismatch

源程序如下：

```
#include <stdio.h>
void main()
{   char s1[80],s2[40]; int j;
    /***** 1 *****/
    int i=0;
    printf("Input the first string:");
    gets(s1);
    printf("Input the second string:");
    gets(s2);
    /********** 2 ********/
    while(s1[i]!='\0')
        i++;
    for(j=0;s2[j]!='\0';j++)
```

11

```
    /****** 3 ******/
    s1[i++] = s2[j];
    /****** 4 ******/
    s1[i+j] = "\0";
    puts(s1);
}
```

如 Figure 1-11 所示,错误提示 1:[error]D:\ccx\gc11.cpp:17:assignment to 'char' from 'const char' lacks a cast.

解析:错误在 D 盘 ccx 文件夹中 gc11.cpp 的 c 程序的第 17 行中,从"const char"(常量字符)到"char"(字符)的分配缺少强制转换,实际上是因为一个字符数组单个单元中只能放一个字符,字符是一定要用单引号包含的,双引号包含的是字符串。

改正:将"\0"改为'\0'即可。

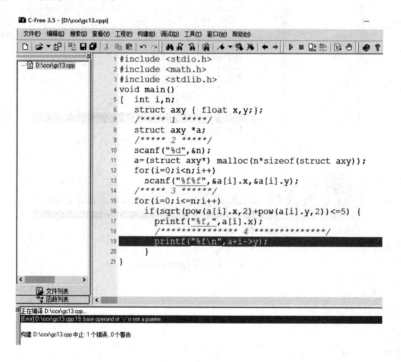

Figure 1-12 Use problem with "->"

源程序如下:
```
#include <stdio.h>
#include <math.h>
#include <stdlib.h>
void main()
{   int i,n;
    struct axy { float x,y;};
    /***** 1 *****/
    struct axy *a;
```

```
/***** 2 *****/
scanf("%d",&n);
a=(struct axy *)malloc(n*sizeof(struct axy));
for(i=0;i<n;i++)
   scanf("%f%f",&a[i].x,&a[i].y);
/***** 3 ******/
for(i=0;i<=n;i++)
   if(sqrt(pow(a[i].x,2)+pow(a[i].y,2))<=5){
      printf("%f,",a[i].x);
      /************** 4 **************/
      printf("%f\n",a+i->y);
   }
}
```

如 Figure 1-12 所示，错误提示 1：[error]D:\ccx\gc13.cpp:19:base operand of '->' is not a point。

解析：错误在 D 盘 ccx 文件夹中 gc13.cpp 的 c 程序的第 19 行中，"—>"的基本操作数不是指针，实际上按照优先级别是先"—>"后"+"，所以是 i—>y，这是非法的，本意是 a+i 中的成员 y。

改正：将 a+i—>y 改为(a+i)—>y 即可。

1.2　软件安装设置错误

如 Figure 1-13 所示，这个错误和前面的都不一样，是编译器错误 compiler error，这个

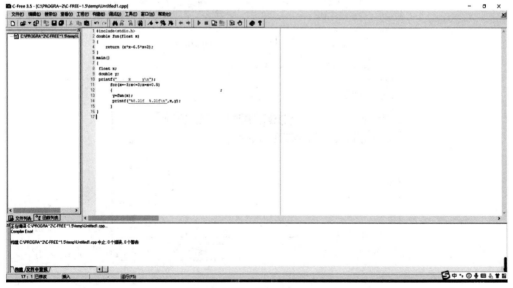

Figure 1-13　Compiler error

错误产生的原因很多，不过在 C-free 中，发生概率最大的原因是设置问题，简单来说就是目录的设置问题。比如，我们可以在"构建→设置"中选择"目录"选项卡，并将里面的 3 个目录路径设置依次截图出来，分别如 Figure 1-14、Figure 1-15、Figure 1-16 所示。

Figure 1-14　Directory of include

Figure 1-15　Directory of executable

Figure 1-16　Directory of library

我们再将上面显示的文件夹路径截图出来，如 Figure 1-17 所示。

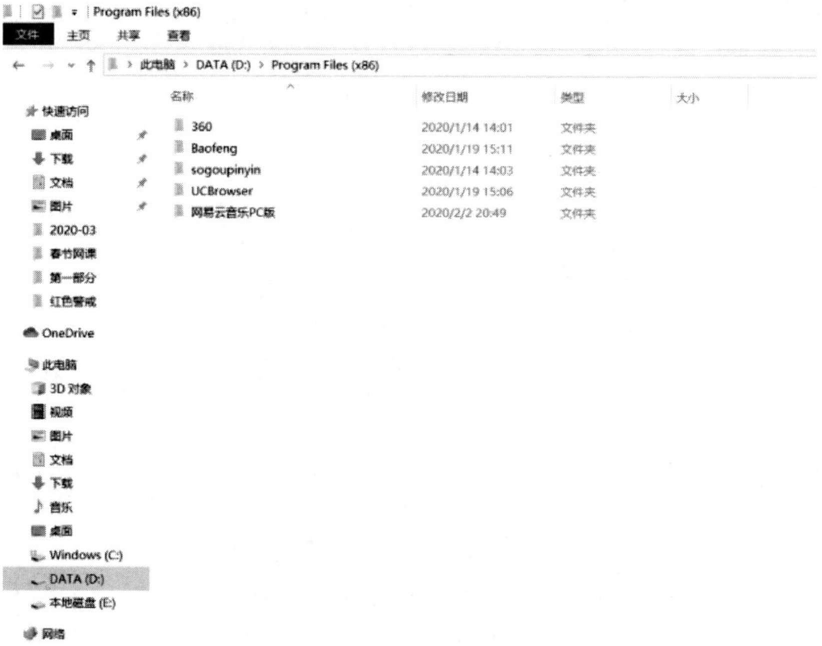

Figure 1-17　The contents of the corresponding file

从 Figure 1-17 可以看出，在设置的对应目录下根本没有对应的文件夹，一般如果正常完成安装的话，该文件夹是正常存在于默认位置的，如 Figure 1-18 所示，并且在各个文件夹下均有对应内容，如 Figure 1-19、Figure 1-20 和 Figure 1-21 所示。我们只要将目录位置改为对应的位置就好。

Figure 1-18　Correct path

电子信息专业英语

Figure 1-19　Correct file 1　　　　　　Figure 1-20　Correct file 2

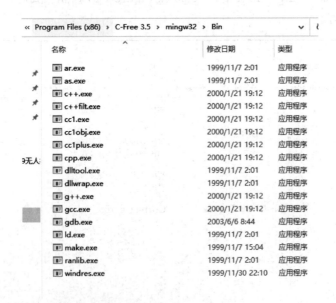

Figure 1-21　Correct file 3

第 2 章 汽车专业英语

2.1 汽车简介

2.1.1 你能说出多少种车的英文名字?

1. 乘用车

(1) 斜背式

A notchback sedan is a three-box sedan, where the passenger volume(容量、体积) is clearly distinct from the trunk volume of the vehicle. The roof is on one plane, generally parallel to the ground, the rear window at a sharp angle to the roof, and the trunk lid is also parallel to the ground. Historically, this has been a popular and arguably(可论证地) the most traditional form of passenger vehicle.

斜背式轿车是三厢式轿车,如 Figure 2-1 所示,其载客量明显不同于车辆的后备厢体积。车顶在一个平面上,通常与地面平行,后车窗与车顶成锐角,行李箱盖也与地面平行。从历史上看,这一直是最受欢迎且最传统的乘用车形式。

Figure 2-1　Notchback

(2) 快背式

快背式是一种车顶轮廓线呈流线型一直连贯至车尾的设计。

A fastback sedan is a two-box sedan, with continuous slope from the roof to the base of the decklid(行李箱盖), but excludes the hatchback feature.

快背式轿车是两厢式轿车,如 Figure 2-2 所示,从车顶到行李箱盖的底部连续倾斜,但不包括掀背车功能。

Figure 2-2　Fastback

（3）掀背式

Hatchback sedans typically have the fastback profile（侧面轮廓）, but instead of a trunk lid, the entire back of the vehicle lifts up（using a liftgate or hatch）.

掀背式轿车通常具有快背轮廓，但不是用行李箱盖，而是用举升门或舱口盖抬高了车辆的整个后部。

Figure 2-3　hatchback

（4）双门轿车

双门轿车（轿跑车）如 Figure 2-4 所示，现在也开始有四门的轿车了。

Figure 2-4　Coupe

（5）活顶乘用车

活顶乘用车（敞篷轿车）如 Figure 2-5 所示。

Figure 2-5　Convertible

（6）高级乘用车

高级乘用车如 Figure 2-6 所示。

Figure 2-6　Pullman saloon

（7）越野车

越野车如 Figure 2-7 所示。

Figure 2-7　Off-road

（8）运动型多用途车

运动型多用途车如 Figure 2-8 所示。

Figure 2-8　SUV(Sports utility vehicle)

（9）多用途车

多用途车 Figure 2-9 集轿车、旅行车和厢式货车的功能于一身，车内每个座椅都可调整，并有多种组合的方式，例如，可将中排座椅靠背翻下即可变为桌台，前排座椅可做 180 度旋转等。近年来，MPV 趋向于小型化，并出现了所谓的 S-MPV，S 是小（small）的意思。S-MPV 车长一般在 4.2 m～4.3 m 之间，车身紧凑，一般为 5～7 座。

Figure 2-9　MPV(Multi purpose vehicle)

（10）休闲车/露营车

休闲车如 Figure 2-10 所示。

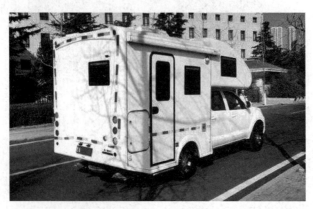

Figure 2-10　RV(recreation vehicle)

(11) 赛车

赛车如 Figure 2-11 所示。

Figure 2-11　Racing car

(12) 皮卡车

皮卡车(轻型卡车)如 Figure 2-12 所示。

Figure 2-12　Pickup

(13) 跨界车

跨界车(Figure 2-13)的车型源自轿车化的运动型多功能车 SUV(sports utility vehicle),逐渐发展成为轿车、SUV、MPV 等车型的任意交叉组合,集轿车的舒适性和时尚外观、SUV 的操控性和 MPV 的自由空间于一身,又有 SUV 的良好通过性与安全性,在空间上也比传统的轿车大很多。跨界车于 20 世纪末起源于日本,之后在北美、西欧等地区流行,英文简写为 CUV(crossover utility vehicle)。

(14) 客货两用车

A station wagon or estate car is a body style variant of a sedan/saloon with its roof extended rearward over a shared passenger/cargo(货物) volume with access at the back via a third or fifth door (the liftgate or tailgate), instead of a trunk lid. The body style transforms a standard three-box design into a two-box design.

Figure 2-13　Crossover vehicle

　　旅行车或小型客车(Figure 2-14)是轿车(美)/轿车(英)的车身样式变体,其车顶向后延伸到共享的乘客/货物容积上,可通过第 3 或第 5 扇门(升降门或后挡板)而不是后备厢门从后部进入。车身样式将标准的三框设计转换为两框设计。

Figure 2-14　Station wagon

2. 商用车

(1) 客车

客车如 Figure 2-15 所示。

Figure 2-15　Bus

（2）单层公共汽车/双层公共汽车

Figure 2-16 是双层公共汽车的图示。

Figure 2-16　Double deck bus

（3）铰接式公交车

铰接式公交车如 Figure 2-17 所示。

Figure 2-17　Articulated bus

（4）低地板公交车

低地板公交车如 Figure 2-18 所示。

Figure 2-18　Low floor bus

（5）小型客车

小型客车如 Figure 2-19 所示。

Figure 2-19　Minibus

（6）公共巴士

Bus used for short-distance public transport purposes.

公共巴士用于短距离的公共运输。

（7）Coach:客车 长途汽车

Coach used to refer to a large motor vehicle for conveying(运送、运输)passengers. To differentiate from other types of bus，a coach has a luggage hold separate from the passenger cabin.

客车指运送乘客的大型汽车。为了与其他类型的公共汽车区分开,教练的行李架与乘客舱分开。

① 长途客车 interurban coach

② 观光客车 touring coach

（8）货车、卡车

Truck（see figure 2-20）used for carrying goods and materials.

Figure 2-20　Truck

(9) 拖车

① 拖车

Trailer(figure 2-21) is an unpowered vehicle pulled by a powered vehicle.

拖车是被动力车辆牵引的无动力车辆。

Figure 2-21　Tractor

② 半挂车

Semi-trailer(figure 2-22) is a trailer without a front axle. A large proportion of its weight is supported either by a road tractor.

半挂车指没有前轴的拖车。它的大部分重量都由公路牵引车支撑。

Figure 2-22　Semi-trailer

(10) 特种车

① 邮政车

邮政车如 Figure 2-23 所示。

Figure 2-23　Mail car

② 洒水车

Figure 2-24 是洒水车。

Figure 2-24　Street sprinkler

③ 警车

Figure 2-25 是警车的图示。

Figure 2-25　Police car

④ 搅拌车

Figure 2-26 为搅拌车。

Figure 2-26　Agitator truck

⑤ 挖掘机

Figure 2-27 为挖掘机。

Figure 2-27　Excavator

⑥ 消防车

Figure 2-28 为消防车。

Figure 2-28　Fire engine

2.1.2　各种汽车

Cars of today have developed into many different body styles befitting their varied uses. Some of these styles are listed below:

Three-door hatchback car, four-door car, five-door hatchback car, two-door hard top and two-door soft top cars, four-door hard top sedan, station wagon, pickup, van and off-road sport cars.

The best style for you depends on the use to which you'll put the car, where you live, the amount of driving you do, your financial resources, and your personal tastes. The most common family automobiles are divided into many styles and are available in four basic sizes: subcompact, compact, intermediate, and full-size.

Subcompacts

Cars of this size often have the lowest original cost and deliver the best fuel(燃料、燃油)economy. Subcompacts generally provide the best handling and easiest maneuvering and parking. However, due to their shorter wheelbase(车轴距)(distance from center of front wheel to center of rear wheel) and their lighter weight, subcompacts give a somewhat firmer ride, which some people prefer. Subcompacts have three, four or five doors and are designed to seat four passengers comfortably. Current subcompact hatchbacks are no more than 4 000 mm long. In addition, many people find themselves crowded inside a subcompact, especially sometimes in the minuscule back seats(后座).

Despite their impressive gas mileage figures, however, subcompact overall maintenance(维护、保养)cost can sometimes run higher than their larger counterparts. This is due partly to the often cramped quarters in which engine parts are installed(安装). Repairing parts cost more, too, particularly for the imported cars(进口轿车).

Examples of subcompact cars as figure 2-29, figure 2-30, figure 2-31, figure 2-32.

Figure 2-29 Ford: Fiesta(3 970 mm)

Figure 2-30 Nissan: Micra(3 779 mm)

Figure 2-31 BYD: F0(3 460 mm)

Figure 2-32 Chery: QQ(3 564 mm)

Compacts

These models are a little larger than subcompacts. They give additional room in the front and rear seats as well as added crash-protection for passengers(乘客). Original cost is somewhat higher than that for the subcompacts. Fuel economy is comparable and maintenance access is easier. Their somewhat roomier nature and better ride often make compacts the choice of the economy-minded driver. Compacts are around 4 200 mm long in case of hatchbacks and 4 600 mm in the case of 4-door cars. Compacts have room for five adults and usually have 4-cylinder engine. These are the most popular vehicles in our country.

Examples of compact cars see figure 2-33,figure 2-34,figure 2-35,figure 2-36.

Figure 2-33　Ford：Focus(4 480 mm)　　　Figure 2-34　Toyota：Corolla(4 555 mm)

Figure 2-35　Volkswagen：Sagetta(4 644 mm)　　　Figure 2-36　Volkswagen：Golf7(4 255 mm)

Intermediates

Also called mid-sized cars, intermediates provide what many consider to be the best trade-off between economy and comfort. Parking maneuverability and fuel economy are superior to the full-size models, while maintenance access, roominess and long-trip comfort are better than those of the compacts and subcompacts. Intermediates have room for five adults and a large trunk (boot). Engines are more powerful than compact cars and 6-cylinder engines are more common than in smaller cars. Car sizes vary from region to region; in Europe, large family cars are rarely over 4 700 mm long, while in North America they may be well over 4 800 mm.

Examples of intermediate cars see figure 2-37,figure 2-38,figure 2-39,figure 2-40.

Figure 2-37   Toyota: Camery(4 825 mm)

Figure 2-38   Volkswagen: Magotan(4 865 mm)

Figure 2-39   FAW: Besturn B90(4 860 mm)

Figure 2-40   Volvo S60(4 715 mm)

Full-sizes

A full-size is typically a four-door car. These cars are the most powerful, with eight and twelve-cylinder engines, so-called gas guzzlers and have more facilities than smaller models. Interior roominess makes them the most comfortable cars for long trips. They're still readily available in the new car marketplace. Full-size cars may be well over 5 000 mm long and are the roomiest vehicles.

Examples of full-size cars see figure 2-41, figure 2-42, figure 2-43, figure 2-44.

Figure 2-41   FAW: H7(5 095 mm)

Figure 2-42   Volkswagen: Audi A8(5 267 mm)

Figure 2-43   BMW7 Series(5 223 mm)

Figure 2-44   Mercedes Benz S-Class(5 250 mm)

New Words and Expressions

befit [bi'fit]	v. 适合,适宜,合式
varied ['vɛərid]	adj. 各种各样的
hatchback ['hætʃ'bæk]	n. 仓门式汽车
sedan [si'dæn]	n. (美)轿车
hardtop ['hɑːrdtɑːp]	n. 金属顶盖敞篷汽车
pickup ['pikʌp]	n. 皮卡,小卡车
financial [fai'nænʃəl]	adj. 金融的,财政的
subcompact ['sʌb'kɔmpækt]	n. 超小型汽车
compact ['kɔmpækt]	adj. 紧凑的,紧密的 n. 紧凑型汽车
intermediate [intə'miːdiət]	adj. 中级的
full-size ['ful'saiz]	adj. 全长的
maneuvering [mə'nuːvəriŋ]	n. 操纵
wheelbase ['wiːlbeis]	n. 前后轮之车轮轴距离,轴距
minuscule [mi'nʌskjuːl]	adj. 微小的,小写字的
counterpart ['kauntəpɑːt]	n. 相似之物
cramped [kræmpt]	adj. 狭窄的,拥挤的
crash-protection [kræʃprə'tekʃən]	n. 防撞击装置
trade-off [treidɔːf]	n. 权衡,取舍
comparable ['kɔmpərəbl]	adj. 可比较的,比得上的
roominess ['ruːminis]	n. 宽敞,广阔
trunk [trʌŋk]	n. (汽车后部)行李箱
boot [buːt]	n. [英]汽车行李箱
choice [tʃɔis]	adj. 上等的,精选的 n. 选择
guzzler ['gʌzlə]	n. 油老虎
interior [in'tiəriə]	adj. 内部的
readily ['redili]	adj. 迅速地,轻易地
soft top	软顶敞篷汽车
station wagon	小旅行车,旅行轿车
original cost	原始成本,原价,原值
fuel economy	节约燃料
gas mileage	一加仑汽油所行驶的里程
maintenance cost	维修费用,维修成本,保养费
be superior to	比……更优越,优于,胜过
maintenance access	维修空间
4-cylinder engine	4缸发动机
Chery	奇瑞,奇瑞汽车
Toyota	丰田,丰田汽车

FAW	一汽
Ford	福特,福特公司,福特汽车
Nissan	尼桑,日产汽车,日产
Volkswagen	大众,大众汽车,大众汽车公司

2.1.3 安全带

听力 2-1

Until children car passengers are tall enough to wear a normal seat belt, they need to use a child seat. The importance of this has been highlighted recently by the National Highway Traffic Safety Administration of the US. They found using these seats can reduce fatal injuries in car crash by up to 71 percent. Yet in China few parents use these potentially life-saving seats.

Here, it's common to see children in the front seat of a car on an adult's lap, or sitting freely in the back seat. If parents were aware of the recently released statistics in the US, would they change their ways? We asked a number of Chinese parents their views on driving with children. "I put him in the front of the car. It's safer this way, because he's next to me." "My child likes to wriggle around so I think it's safer to hold him on my lap." "I tell my kid to sit in the back with the seatbelt fastened. This should be safe." But experts warn of tragic results because of such habits. Sitting a child in the front of a car could be very dangerous. Children can be injured by the airbags suddenly inflating during a crash.

Holding the child is also a bad idea. The inertia generated in a crash can multiply a child's weight thirty times making it impossible for a parent to keep hold.

听力原文译文

直到儿童汽车乘客高到足以系上普通安全带之前,他们都需要使用儿童座椅。美国国家公路交通安全管理局最近强调了这一点的重要性。他们发现使用这些座椅可以减少多达71%的车祸致命伤害。但是在中国,很少有父母会使用这些可能挽救生命的座椅。

在这里,通常会看到孩子在汽车前排座位坐在大人的大腿上,或者自由地坐在后排座位上。如果父母知道美国最近发布的统计数据,他们会改变自己的方式吗?我们询问了许多中国父母对带孩子开车的看法。"我把他放在车前。这样比较安全,因为他在我旁边。""我的孩子喜欢四处走动,所以我认为将他抱在腿上比较安全。""我告诉我的孩子坐在座位上,系好安全带。这应该是安全的。"但是专家警告,这种习惯会导致悲剧性的结果。让孩子坐在汽车前可能很危险。在碰撞期间,安全气囊突然膨胀可能会伤及儿童。

抱着孩子也是一个坏主意。碰撞中产生的惯性会使孩子的体重增加三十倍,使得父母根本无法抱住他。

2.2 汽车标志

2.2.1 今日最受欢迎的汽车品牌

Figure 2-45、Figure 2-46 为如今最受欢迎的汽车品牌。

Figure 2-45 Car brands 1

Figure 2-46 Car brands 2

2.2.2 你认识这些汽车品牌吗?

Geely(see figure 2-47), a private company, built in 1985, mainly focused on automobile and motor. It built Geely College in 2000 and donated 18 million in Wenchuan Earthquake. Since 2009, Geely is the owner of VOLVO. To the meaning of Geely, the circle is the earth and the picture in the middle of the logo is six "6", meaning smooth going and good fortune.

Figure 2-47 Geely

吉利(见 Figure 2-47)是一家成立于 1985 年的私企,主要生产汽车和发动机。2000 年创建吉利大学,并且在汶川地震中资助 1 800 万元。2009 年,吉利收购了沃尔沃。对于吉利标志的含义,圆代表了地球,六个"6"标志着顺利和好运。

Figure 2-48　BMW

BMW, see figure 2-48, the whole name is Bayerische Motoren Werke AG (in German). BMW Group, one of the fortune 500 companies, is the world's most successful and profitable automobile and motorcycle manufacturers.

宝马,如 Figure 2-48 所示,全名是 Bayerische Motoren Werke AG(德语)。宝马集团是世界 500 强企业之一,是全球最成功、最赚钱的汽车和摩托车制造商。

The BMW logo is a rounded, stylized representation of a spinning propeller blade. (The company built military airplane engines originally.)

宝马的车标是一个被圆包围的旋转着的螺旋桨叶片。(该公司原本是生产军用飞机引擎的。)

Bavaria's state flag is blue and white. BMW's name is Bavarian Motor Works (in English), on behalf of the Bavarian BMW and represents Germany's most exquisite engine technology.

巴伐利亚的州旗是蓝色和白色。宝马的名字叫 Bavarian Motor Works(英文),代表 Bavarian(巴伐利亚)的宝马,代表了德国最精致的发动机技术。

One of the reasons to BMW's success is the proper marketing strategy. First, meet different consumer groups. For example, 3 Series locate the young, sports and 8 Series locate super luxury sports car. Second, high quality and price. Of course, it also means that the status of the BMW brand and reputation. BMW's prices are generally 10% to 20% higher than the same cars.

宝马成功的原因之一是正确的营销策略。首先,迎合不同的消费群体。例如,3 系列定位年轻,运动型和 8 系列定位超级豪华跑车。其次,它拥有高品质。当然,这也意味着宝马的品牌和声誉。宝马的价格通常比同类汽车高 10%至 20%。

The four rings is the Audi logo (see figure 2-49) and represent the four companies of the Auto-Union consortium of 1932—DKW, Horch, Wanderer, and Audi. The Audi's name (Latin for "Hear!") disappeared after WWII, but was revived in 1965. Audi group consists of the parent company and its subsidiary company, Audi Hungarian company, Quattro limited company and Automobili Lamborghini S. P. A. and Cosworth technology company. In 1932, Audi and DKW, Horch and Wanderer merged into the Auto Union

Company, and start using ring logo. In 1966, Audi became subcompany of FAW Volkswagen.

奥迪车标(如 Figure 2-49 所示)的四个连环代表 1932 年组成汽车联盟股份公司的四家公司——小奇迹(DKW)、霍希(Horch)、漫游者(Wanderer)和奥迪(Audi)公司。奥迪这个名字(拉丁语里面是"听到"的意思)在二战后停用,而在 1965 年被重新启用。奥迪集团包括母公司及其子公司奥迪匈牙利公司、Quattro 有限公司以及兰博基尼汽车公司和 Cosworth 技术公司。1932 年,奥迪与小奇迹、霍希和漫游者合并成的汽车联盟公司开始采用四环徽标,并于 1966 年成为大众公司的子公司。

Figure 2-49   Audi

The Toyota logo(see figure 2-50) is comprised of three ellipses, representing the heart of the customer, the heart of the product, and the ever expanding technological advancements and opportunities that lie ahead. Another interpretation is that it represents the three interlocking aspects of the culture of the company—freedom, team spirit, and progress. Also, in Japanese "Toyo" means an abundance of, and "ta" is rice. In some Asian cultures, those blessed with an abundance of rice are believed to be blessed with great wealth.

丰田的车标(如 Figure 2-50 所示)有三个椭圆组成,分别代表消费者的心、产品的心和不断进步的技术及发展良机。另一种说法是它代表了公司文化的三个紧密关联的方面——自由、团队精神和进步。在日语里,"Toyo"意为充足,而"ta"为大米。在一些亚洲文化中,拥有大量大米的人就意味着拥有了巨大财富。

Figure 2-50   Toyota

Toyota Motor Corporation, commonly known simply as Toyota, is a multinational corporation and head quartered in Japan. Toyota today uses a logo which has three ovals. The two perpendicular inner ovals stand for mutual trust between the customer and the Toyota Company. The two ovals also symbolize the letter "T" for Toyota. The bigger outer oval stands for the worldwide expansion of Toyota's technology and endless potential for the future.

丰田汽车公司,常被称为丰田,是一家跨国公司,总部设在日本。丰田的标志包括三个椭圆。两个垂直相交的椭圆表示汽车制造者与顾客心心相印,并且,横竖两椭圆组合在一起,表示丰田(Toyota)的第一个字母T。外圈大点的椭圆代表丰田在世界范围内的先进技术和未来的无限潜力。

The history of Lamborghini Automobili officially starts in 1963. Nevertheless, we must consider the far-off roots of this event, and they are the roots of Ferruccio Lamborghini. The Lamborghini's Bull Logo (see figure 2-51) stands for the founder's, Ferruccio Lamborghini, zodiacal sign (Taurus). Born in 1916, this capable, impetuous, strong-willed Taurus was the leading character in the foundation of the company and the early phases of its extraordinary history.

兰博基尼汽车公司的历史正式开始于1963年。然而,我们必须考虑这一事件根源,那就是源于费鲁吉欧·兰博基尼。兰博基尼的公牛标志(见Figure 2-51)代表着创建者费鲁吉欧·兰博基尼。他出生于1916年,这个有能力、迅猛、意志坚强的金牛是该公司的基础,是其非凡历史早期阶段的主角。

Figure 2-51 Lamborghini

The founder of Lamborghini, Ferrucio Lamborghini, had a passion of bull fighting, as evidenced by the logo chosen for his car company—a charging bull. Mr. Lamborghini also carried this theme over to the names of his cars, almost all of which were named after either a breed of fighting bull or a particular bull.

兰博基尼汽车的创立人弗鲁西欧·兰博基尼(Ferrucio Lamborghini)是斗牛运动的爱好者,这一点可以从他为汽车公司选择的车标———一头进攻的公牛———得到证明。兰博基尼先生也把斗牛的主题延伸到他的汽车名称上,他所有的汽车几乎都是以某一头公牛或某一头好斗的公牛的品种来命名的。

Rolls-Royce   劳斯莱斯(德国)

Rolls-Royce, see figure 2-52, is a manufacturer of the top luxury car, which was founded in 1906 in England. The company founders were Frederick Henry Royce and Charles Stewart Rolls and their car is an excellent representative of the world's top-level cars. Rolls-Royce car is famous for its luxury configuration and pure manual production.

The luxury(奢侈) materials, exquisite craft and expensive labor costs determine the high price of the car. As its yield is very low, it is a symbol of identity and status that owning a Rolls-Royce car.

Figure 2-52　Rolls-Royce

劳斯莱斯(Rolls-Royce),如 Figure 2-52 所示,是顶级豪华汽车的制造商,该豪华汽车于 1906 年在英格兰成立。该公司的创始人是弗雷德里克·亨利·罗伊斯和查尔斯·斯图尔特·劳斯,他们的汽车是世界顶级汽车的杰出代表。劳斯莱斯汽车以其豪华的配置和纯手工生产而闻名。豪华的材料、精湛的工艺和昂贵的人工成本决定了汽车的高昂价格。由于收益率很低,因此拥有劳斯莱斯汽车是身份和地位的象征。

Frederick Henry Royce was born into a miller's family, in 1863. He worked as a apprentice at an early age, but through efforts he became an electrical engineer of the company at the age of 19. He had a very high mechanical talents, strives for perfection, and designed and manufactured his own car by himself in 1904.

弗雷德里克·亨利·罗伊斯(Frederick Henry Royce)于 1863 年出生于磨坊家庭。他很小的时候就当学徒,但是通过努力,他在 19 岁时成为公司的电气工程师。他拥有非常高的机械才能,追求完美,并于 1904 年亲自设计和制造了自己的汽车。

In 1877, Charles Stewart Rolls was born in noble family, and graduated from the university of Cambridge. He was not only personable, but also mastered of driving.

查尔斯·斯图尔特·劳斯(Charles Stewart Rolls)于 1877 年出身于贵族家庭,毕业于剑桥大学。他不仅风度翩翩,而且精通驾驶。

In 1904, the two men who both had ambition with car met in Manchester. They successfully established a cooperative relationship and in the same year they founded the Rolls-Royce motor company. Two years later, their production Rolls-Royce Silver Ghost was hailed as the best car in the world.

1904 年,两个对汽车充满野心的男人在曼彻斯特相识。他们成功建立了合作关系,并于同年成立了劳斯莱斯汽车公司。两年后,他们生产的劳斯莱斯银魅被誉为世界上最好的汽车。

The Rolls-Royce logo consists of double "R" which apparently stands for Rolls and Royce. Though the Rolls Royce logo was simply designed, the name is so powerful that the

Rolls Royce logo looks attractive and distinctive. That's because "the hyphen" symbolizes the partnership or the link between the two founders. "The Spirit of Ecstasy" or "The Flying Lady" is also an important element of Rolls Royce.

劳斯莱斯徽标由双"R"组成，代表了"Rolls and Royce"。尽管劳斯莱斯的徽标设计简单，但名字如此有力，以至于劳斯莱斯徽标看起来引人注目和独特，这是因为"连字符"象征两个创立者的伙伴关系，"欢庆女神"或"飞天女神"也是劳斯莱斯的重要元素。

2.2.3　汽车制造商徽标

Different vehicles have different logos. Logo is the symbol of an automaker or a series of automobiles. Let's get familiar with some of the famous logos of automakers in the world.

不同的车辆有着不同的车标。车标是一个汽车制造商或一系列车辆的象征。让我们一起来熟悉一下世界上一些著名汽车制造商的汽车标志吧。

I'm sure that you must have seen these trademarks（商标）（see figure 2-53）on streets. They are all the logos of American automakers. The left one is the logo of GM Company, the right one belongs to the Chrysler Company, while the middle one is the symbol of Ford Company. Their products have been in the Chinese market for a long time, and they all have joint ventures with the Chinese auto enterprises.

我相信你们一定在大街上见过以下这些车的车标，如 Figure 2-53 所示。他们都是美国汽车制造商的车标。左边的是通用公司的汽车标志，右边的车标属于克莱斯勒公司，中间的是福特公司的标志。他们的产品投入中国市场已经有很长一段时间了，并且他们都与中国的汽车企业进行合资。

Figure 2-53　GM Ford chrysler

You will not be unfamiliar with these trademarks. "VW" is the abbreviation（缩写）of the "Volkswagen", a German automobile manufacturer. More and more Chinese are getting to know this company. Since the establishment of the first joint venture in Shanghai, Volkswagen has made great progress in developing the Chinese market. Now VW maintains good cooperation with Chinese enterprises. Nearly 30% of the cars you see on the street are products of VW. From the early Santana to the latest Audi A8, from Golf, Jetta to Baro and Passat, VW（figure 2-54）has become a symbol of speed, safety and ease.

下边的这些车标你一定不会感到陌生。"VW"是德国汽车制造商大众的缩写。越来越多的中国人开始了解这个名字。自从在上海建立第一家合资企业以来,大众在占领中国市场方面取得了很大的进步。现在的大众公司和中国的企业保持着良好的合作关系。你在大街上看到的汽车几乎有 30% 都是大众公司生产的。从早期的桑塔纳到最新的奥迪 A8,从高尔夫、捷达到宝来和帕萨特,大众车(如 Figure 2-54 所示)已经成为速度、安全和舒适的象征。

Figure 2-54　Audi Volkswagen skoda

The following trademarks belong to some French auto companies. The left one is the logo of Peugeot Company, the right one the logo of Citroen Company, while the middle logo is the symbol of Renault Group. As big auto dealers in European market, they are all famous for their sedan products.

下列车标属于法国汽车公司。左边是标致公司的汽车标志,右边是雪铁龙的车标,中间的车标属于雷诺集团。作为欧洲市场实力强大的汽车商,他们都以其轿车产品而闻名。

Figure 2-55　Peugeot Renault Citroen

I'm sure that you are familiar with these trademarks. Yes, they are the logos of several Chinese automakers. The left one in the first row has a very beautiful name, the AELOUS(风神), which is the logo of DONGFENG Group. This company is engaged in producing trucks and passenger cars. The right one in the first row belongs to Beijing Jeep Corporation. This company has focused on producing jeeps over these years. And now it's famous for the Cherokee serial jeeps, as a co-produced enterprise with Chrysler, USA. There are also some other logos of Chinese automakers below in figure 2-56.

非常确信你一定非常熟悉下面的车标。是的,他们是一些中国汽车公司的车标。第一行左边的车标有一个非常美丽的名字,"风神",它是东风集团的标志。这个公司致力于生产卡车和客车。第一行右边的车标属于北京吉普集团。北京吉普集团公司多年来一直致力于生产吉普车。作为克莱斯勒公司的合作伙伴,它以切诺基系列而闻名。Figure 2-56 是一些中国其他汽车生产商的汽车标志。

Figure 2-56　The logos of several Chinese automakers

New Words and Expressions

Intelligent [ɪnˈtelɪdʒənt]　　　　adj. 聪明的,有智力的,智能的
logo [ˈləʊɡəʊ]　　　　　　　　n. 图形,商标,标识语
automaker [ˈɔːtəʊmeɪkə]　　　n. 汽车制造商
abbreviation [əˌbriːvɪˈeɪʃən]　　n. 缩写,缩写词,缩写形式
cooperation [kəʊɔpəreɪʃən]　　n. 合作,协作,协助,配合
vehicle [ˈviːɪkl]　　　　　　　　n. 交通工具,车辆,传播媒介,手段
trademark [ˈtreɪdmɑːk]　　　　n. (注册)商标
dealer [ˈdiːlə]　　　　　　　　n. 商人,贩毒者,毒品贩子
joint [dʒɔɪnt]　　　　　　　　adj. 共同的,联合的
venture [ˈventʃə]　　　　　　　n. (商业)冒险,冒险行动
enterprise [ˈentəpraɪz]　　　　n. 企业,公司,事业,计划
establishment [ɪsˈtæblɪʃmənt]　n. 建立,确立
maintain [meɪnˈteɪn]　　　　　vt. 保持,保存,维持,持续,使继续
get / be familiar with …　　　　熟悉
belong to …　　　　　　　　　属于,为……之一员
more and more …　　　　　　越来越……

2.2.4　车标轶事

Figure 2-57 是一些车标。

Figure 2-57　Car brands

　　The Alfa Romeo logo represents the coat of arms of the city of Milan and is related to the Crusades(十字军东征), hence the cross. On the right, a snake is eating a figure; either a child or a Saracen, it depends on who you ask.

　　阿尔法·罗密欧的车标是米兰城的盾形徽章,与十字军东征有关,所以有十字架图案。右边是一条蛇正在吞噬人形,有人说是小孩,也有人说是撒拉逊人,不同的人有不同的说法。

　　Buick's logo originated from the coat of arms of the Buick family (of Scottish origin); a red shield with a checkered silver and azure(天蓝色的、蔚蓝色的) diagonal(对角线的斜线的) line running from the upper left corner of the shield and a gold cross in the lower left corner (the cross had a hole in the center with the red of the shield showing through), and in the upper right corner was an antlered(鹿角) deer head with a jagged neckline. The logo underwent many revisions, and then in 1959 the logo was changed to three shields, to represent the three Buick models in production at the time (LeSabre, Invicta, and

Electra)。

别克的车标源自别克家族(苏格兰血统)的家徽,是一个红色盾形标志,从左上角开始有一个银色和天蓝色格子的带状图案。左下角有一个金色十字架(十字架中间有一圆孔,透过此可见红色的盾牌),右上角是带有锯齿状领圈的长有鹿角的鹿头。别克车标几经修改,在1959年改成了三个盾牌的样子,分别代表当时正在生产的三款别克车(LeSabre,Invicta,和Electra)。

The original Cadillac logo is based on the family crest(饰章)of the man for whom the company was named, Antoine de La Mothe, Sieyr de Cadillac, but many believe the crest is a fake, concocted(炮制、杜撰) for the purposes of the company's logo. The symbolism of the wreath surrounding the crest is uncertain, though the original wreath design was a bouquet(花束) of tulip leaves.

凯迪拉克汽车最初的车标是基于公司为之命名的安东尼·门斯·凯迪拉克的家徽的,但许多人认为这是伪造之物,是为了公司的标志而杜撰出来的。花冠盾形车标的象征意义并不明确,不过这花冠的最初式样是一束郁金香的叶子。

Popular legend has it that the Chevrolet logo was inspired by wallpaper in a French hotel where William C. Durant was staying. It says he saw the pattern marching off into infinity as a design on the wallpaper and tore a piece of it off to keep to show to friends and later turn into the company logo. However, his wife says that the bow tie emblem was first seen by her husband in a Virginia newspaper on a vacation around 1912, upon which he told her that the thought would be a very good emblem for the Chevrolet.

一则关于雪佛兰车标比较流行的传奇故事认为,雪佛兰车标的灵感源于威廉·杜兰特(William C. Durant)所住过的一家法国酒店的壁纸。传说他看到壁纸上的图案有一种无限的印象,然后撕了一块下来去给朋友们看,后来变成了雪佛兰车标。但是,他的妻子说这个像领结的标志是她丈夫在1912年左右度假时在一张弗吉尼亚的报纸上看到的,当时他还告诉她这个图案将会是雪佛兰的很好的车标。

The Chrysler logo has undergone quite a few changes over the years; the one shown here is an adaptation of the original medallion logo used on Chrysler cars at its inception in 1925. This logo was brought back to use in 1994, and the pair of silver wings were added after the company merged with Daimler-Benz in 1998. Now that Chrysler's been sold to Cerberus, they're switching back to the Pentastar design, though the cars are still using the logo shown here.

克莱斯勒的车标在过去几年中几经变化,这里的车标是1925年最初在克莱斯勒汽车上使用的大奖章标志的改进版。1944年这标志别重新启用,1998年公司于戴姆勒-奔驰合并时添加了银色双翼。克莱斯勒出售给塞伯鲁斯资本管理公司后,他们转用五角星标志,但其生产的汽车仍沿用此车标。

The Dodge Ram logo first appeared as a hood ornament(装饰品) in the 1930s, used on both trucks and cars. The Ram was chosen for the image it portrays, sure-footed, king of the trail.

道奇的羊头车标在20世纪30年代时作为其汽车和卡车上的车篷装饰使用,因其表现了步伐稳健的跳跃之王形象,而被选为道奇车标。

The prancing horse featured on the Ferrari logo was the emblem of Italian WWI flying ace Fancesco Baracca, whose parents persuaded Enzo Ferrari to use the symbol of their son for his Alfa Romeo race cars. When Ferrari later started his own car company, he continued to use this logo.

法拉利汽车上的腾跃骏马车标是第一次世界大战时意大利空军王牌飞行员佛朗西斯科·巴勒可(Fancesco Baracca)在飞机上使用的标记,他的父母劝说恩佐·法拉利在阿尔法·罗密欧比赛中使用他们儿子飞行时使用的标志。之后,法拉利创建自己的汽车公司时,沿用了这个车标。

Henry Ford's right-hand-man, Harold Wills, printed business cards to earn money as a teen, and when Mr. Ford needed a logo, Wills pulled out his old printing set and used a font that he had used for his own cards. The oval was added in 1912, and blue was added for the Model A in 1927.

亨利·福特的得力助手哈罗德·威尔斯(Harold Wills)在十几岁时通过印刷名片来赚钱。当福特先生想要一个车标时,威尔斯弃用了他的旧印刷样板,使用他曾为他自己的名片使用过的字体,设计了福特字样的标识。椭圆形是在1912年加上去的,而蓝色是在1927年为福特A系列加上去的。

The Infiniti logo is derived from the symbol for infinity, not surprisingly. The concept of the open road and traveling toward infinity was one the company wanted the customer to feel.

毫不奇怪,英菲尼迪的车标源自无限的象征。该公司希望用户借此能体会到广阔的公路和驶向无限的概念。

Originally the Swallow Sidecar Company, Jaguar gained its new name in 1945, though why this particular animal was chosen is uncertain. It's thought the leaping jaguar is meant to represent the speed, power, and quickness of the cars.

捷豹汽车前身为斯瓦罗汽车公司(Swallow Sidecar Company),在1945年才改用新名。为何选中美洲豹这个动物不得而知,但其跳跃前扑的形象传达了汽车的速度、力量和迅捷。

The trident prominent in the Maserati logo is the traditional symbol for Bologna, where the cars were originally made (they're now built in nearby Modena).

玛莎拉蒂车标上显著的三叉戟标志是该汽车原产地博洛尼亚市的传统标志,如今该汽车在靠近博洛尼亚的小城(Modena 摩德纳)生产。

Rei Yoshimara, a world-renowned corporate image-creator, designed the Mazda logo. The "V" represents wings outstretched.

马自达的车标是由世界著名的企业形象设计者Rei Yoshimara设计的,其V形展现了展翅飞翔的形象。

The three-pointed star of Mercedes' logo represents their domination(控制、统治)of land, sea, and air. First used on a Daimler in 1909, a laurel wreath was added in 1926 to signify the union with Benz, and was later simplified to the current logo design in 1937.

梅赛德斯车标中的三叉星分别代表了该公司对土地,海洋和空气的主宰地位。该车标在1909年首次使用在戴姆勒汽车上,在1923年添加了月桂枝以标志戴姆勒公司和奔驰公司的合并,之后在1937年车标被简化为如今的样子。

Some believe that the Mitsubishi logo represents a ship's propeller (Mitsuibishi was involved in shipbuilding early in the company's existence). However, a more commonly accepted explanation is that the logo is formed by the joining of two family emblems and does not represent any part of a ship.

有人认为三菱汽车的车标代表了船舶的螺旋桨(三菱在其创建初期专门造船)。不过,更为大家接受的一种解释认为这个车标是由两个家徽结合而成的,并不代表船舶的任何部分。

The Porsche badge is the coat of arms of the city of Stuttgart where the cars are built. The city was built on the site of a stud farm, which explains the horse in the coat of arms; the antlers and red and black stripes are part of the coat of arms of the Kingdom of Wurttemberg.

保时捷的车标采用该汽车生产地斯图加特市的盾形市徽。该城原址为一个马场,这正好解释车标中使用的马的图案;鹿角和红黑条纹是符腾堡王国盾徽中的部分图案。

Subaru is the first Japanese company to use a name derived from its own language, and that name is reflected in its logo. The name refers to a group of six stars in the constellation of Taurus.

斯巴鲁是第一家使用本国语言来命名的日本公司,而且其名也在其车标中得以体现,指金牛座中的六连星。

The Volkswagen logo is simple, but the name has an interesting meaning——in German, it translates as "People's Car".

大众的车标非常简单,但它的名字很有意思——在德语里面意指"人民的汽车"。

New Words and Expressions

  represent [reprɪzent]   vt. 象征,表示,代表(某人,某团体)
  coat of arms [kəʊt əv ɑːmz]   n. 盾徽,(盾形)纹章
  crusade [kruːseɪd]   n. 十字军东征,改革(讨伐)运动   vi. 加入十字军,从事改革(讨伐)运动
  Saracen [særəsn]   n. 撒拉逊人
  shield [ʃiːld]   n. 盾,盾形纹徽,护盖,挡板   vt. 保护……,掩护,遮蔽
  fake [feɪk]   vt. 伪造,仿造(某物) n. 骗子,赝品
  concoct [kənkɔkt]   vt. 配制,捏造,虚构
  symbolism [sɪmbəlɪzəm]   n. (文学作品等的)象征主义(手法)
  wreath [riːθ]   n. 花圈,(戴在头或颈上的)花冠,花环
  bouquet [bukeɪ]   n. 花束,酒的芳香
  inspire [ɪnspaɪə]   vt. 鼓舞,激励,使产生灵感,启示
  bowtie [bəʊtaɪ]   n. 蝶形领结

emblem [embləm]		n. 徽章，象征，标志
Medallion [mɪdæljən]		n. (挂在颈上的)圆形奖章，大奖牌
sure-footed [ʃʊəfutɪd]		adj. 步子稳的，判断准确的，稳当的
Prance [præns]		vi. (动物)腾跃，欢跃，雀跃
right-hand-man [raɪt hænd mæn]		n. 得力助手
oval [əʊvəl]		adj. 卵形的，椭圆形的
leap [liːp]		vi. 跳跃，敏捷跳动 n. 跳跃，飞跃，数量激增
trident ['traɪdnt]		n. 三叉戟(武器)，三叉状器具
prominent ['prɒmɪnənt]		adj. 凸出的，显著的，杰出的
domination [dɒmə'neɪʃən]		n. 支配，控制，统治，优势
laurel ['lɔːrəl]		n. 月桂树，桂冠，殊荣
badge [bædʒ]		n. 徽章，证章，标记，象征
stud [stʌd]		n. 种马，畜牧场
antler ['æntlə]		n. 鹿角
stripe [straɪp]		n. 条纹，条带，军服上表示等级的条纹
constellation [kɒnstə'leɪʃən]		n. 星座，荟萃，群集
interpretation [ɪntəːprɪ'teɪʃən]		n. 解释，阐明
abundance [ə'bʌndəns]		n. 充裕，丰富
depend on/upon		信赖，凭靠，依赖，依靠
name for/after…		以……的名字起名
a bouquet of		一束……
a piece of		一块，一张，一件，一首，一片
bring back		把……送回，使恢复
merge with…		和……联合、结合、合并
switch back		转回，复原
pull out		(车辆等)驶出，离开，撤离
derive from…		由……而来，从……引申出
build on…		以……为基础，把……建立于
be comprised of…		由……组成
an abundance of		大量的，充裕的
be blessed with		有幸得到
The Crusades		十字军东征
the Auto-Union consortium		奥迪的前身——汽车联盟股份公司
Horch		霍希公司
Audi		奥迪公司
Wanderer		漫游者公司
DKW		小奇迹公司
DKW		小奇迹公司
LeSabre，Invicta，Electra		别克的三种车型

Antoine de La Mothe, Sieyr de Cadillac	安东尼·门斯·凯迪拉克
William C. Durant	威廉·杜兰特,通用汽车公司创始人
Ferrucio Lamborghini	弗鲁西欧·兰博基尼,兰博基尼汽车的创始人
the Kingdom of Wurttemberg	符腾堡王国
Taurus	金牛座

2.3 汽车基础知识

2.3.1 汽车的主要零件是什么?

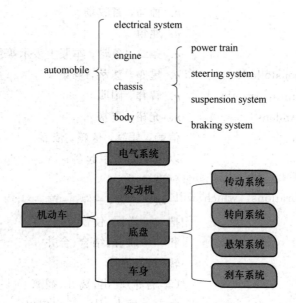

1. 汽车的主要构成

Today's average car contains more than 15 000 separate, individual parts that must work together. These parts can be grouped into four major categories: engine, body, chassis and electrical equipment.

当今的车辆一般都由15 000多个分散独立且相互配合的零部件组成,这些零部件可被归为四大主要类别:发动机、车身、底盘和电气设备。

(1) The engine acts as the power unit. The internal combustion engine is most common: this obtains its power by burning a liquid fuel inside the engine cylinder. There are two types of engine: gasoline(also called a spark-ignition engine) and diesel(also called a compression-ignition engine). Both engines are called heat engines, the burning fuel generates heat which causes the gas inside the cylinder to increase its pressure and supply power to rotate a shaft connected to the transmission.

发动机为汽车提供能源。最常见是内燃机：通过在引擎缸内燃烧液体燃料获得能量。发动机有两种：汽油机（点燃式）和柴油机（压燃式）。两种引擎都叫热机。燃烧的燃料产生热量，使气缸内的气体增加压力并提供动力，使连接到变速器（传动系统）的轴旋转。

(2) An automobile body is a sheet metal shell with windows, doors, a hood, and a trunk deck built into it. It provides a protective covering for the engine, passengers, and cargo. The body is designed to keep passengers safe and comfortable. The body styling provides an attractive, colorful, modern appearance for the vehicle.

车身是金属板壳，由窗户、门、引擎盖、行李盖等组成，它为发动机、乘客及货物提供空间和保护。车身的设计要让乘客安全并乘坐舒适。对于乘用汽车，车身要动感，色彩绚丽，现代化。

(3) The chassis is an assembly of those systems that are the major operating part of a vehicle. The chassis includes the transmission, suspension, steering, and brake systems. Transmission systems — conveys the drive to the wheels. The main components are clutch, gearbox, driveshaft, final drive, and differential. Suspension — absorbs the road shocks. Steering — controls the direction of the movement. Brake — slows down the vehicle.

底盘是一个组合体，主要是汽车的操纵部分，由传动系统、悬架、转向部分、制动系统组成。传动系统用来驱动车轮，主要由离合器、变速箱、驱动轴（传动轴）、主减速器和差速器（分速器）组成。悬架系统主要用来吸收路面冲击。转向系统控制汽车的行驶方向。制动系统使汽车停下来。

The purpose of the complete suspension system is to isolate the vehicle body from road shocks and vibrations, which will otherwise be transferred to the passengers and load. It must also keep the tires in contact with the road regardless of road surface.

悬架系统的作用是隔离来自路面的冲击和振动，防止它们传递给乘客和货物。另外不管路面如何，悬架系统都应该保持轮胎和路面的接触。

Drum brakes have a drum attached to the wheel hub, and braking occurs by means of brake shoes expanding against the inside of the drum. With disc brakes, a disc attached to the wheel hub is clenched between two brake pads.

在鼓式制动器上，制动鼓和轮毂连接，制动蹄张开压紧制动鼓内侧从而产生制动。在盘式制动器上，连接到轮毂的盘被夹紧在两个制动衬块之间。

(4) The electrical system supplies electricity for the ignition, horn, lights, heater, and starter. The electricity level is maintained by a charging circuit. This circuit consists of the battery, alternator (or generator). The battery stores electricity. The alternator changes the engine's mechanical energy into electrical energy and recharges the battery.

电动系统主要为点火器、喇叭、灯、加热器及启动器提供电能。电量由充电电路维持。该电路由电池、交流发电机（或发电机）组成。电池储存电能，发电机把引擎的机械能转化为电能，给电池充电。

2. 下面是汽车的解剖，详见 **Figure 2-58** 和 **Table 2-1**。

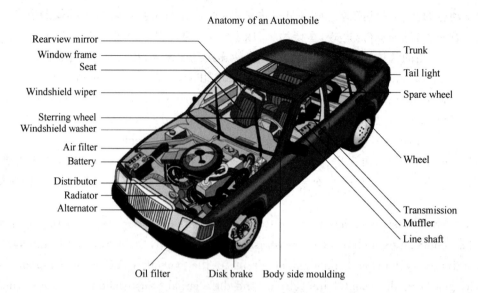

Figure 2-58 The anatomy of an automobile

Table 2-1 Car parts

English Terms	Explanations	Chinese
Automobile	Road vehicle that is motor-driven and is used for transporting people	汽车
Trunk	Place for storing baggage	后备厢
Tail light	Rear light	尾灯
Spare wheel	Wheel of a car used to replace a damaged wheel	备用轮胎
Wheel	Round object that turns around a central axel and allows the car to advance	车轮
Transmission	Automobile apparatus that transmits mechanical power to the wheels	变速器
Muffler	Device used to reduce engine noise	消声器
Drive shaft	Axel on which mechanical power is transmitted to the wheels	传动轴
Body side molding	Decorative molding on the side of a car	车身侧部装饰条
Disk brake	Mechanism that slows and stops a car by friction, by pressing a disk against the axel of a wheel	盘式制动器
Oil filter	Device that removes impurities from oil passing through it	机油滤清器
Alternator	Generator that produces an alternating current	交流电机
Radiator	Apparatus that cools the motor	散热器
Distributor	Case that is used to fire the cylinders	配电器
Battery	Device that generates electric current	蓄电池
Air filter	Device that remove impurities from air passing through it	空气滤清器
Windshield washer	Device used to clean the windows	挡风玻璃清洗器
Steering wheel	Device used to handle a car in conjunction with steering and gear systems	转向盘
Windshield wiper	Movable device, made partly of rubber, that wipes the windshield and rear window of a car	风挡雨刷器

续表

English Terms	Explanations	Chinese
Seat	Type of armchair in the passenger compartment of a car	座椅
Window frame	Border around a window	窗框
Rearview mirror	Inside mirror used for looking backward	后视镜
line shaft	a main shaft usually bearing pulleys by which machines are driven	主传动轴

2.3.2 汽车发动机

The automobile engine is an internal combustion engine which converts the heat energy of fuel into mechanical energy to make the car move.

As the source of power, the engine requires a fuel system to supply it with the mixture of air and fuel or fuel. It plays a vital role in the power-producing process. Suppose the engine is a gasoline engine, the fuel system pumps liquid gasoline from a tank into the carburetor where the gasoline can be mixed with air. The mixture is delivered to the engine where it is burned. If engine is EFI engine, fuel is delivered from the tank to the injector by means of an electric fuel pump. The fuel injectors, which directly control fuel metering to the intake manifold, are pulsed by the ECU. The ECU determines air/fuel ratio of the engine according to engine condition.

The engine also needs a cooling system, because the combustion of the air-fuel mixture in the engine creates a very high temperature (as high as 2 000 to 2 700 ℃). The cooling system takes heat away from the engine by either circulating a liquid coolant (water mixed with antifreeze) between the engine and a radiator, or passing air through the radiator. Today, liquid-cooled engines are common. It cools off as it goes through the radiator. Thus, the coolant continually takes heat away from the engine, where it could do damage and delivers it to the radiator.

The engine also includes a lubricating system. The purpose of the lubricating system is to supply all moving parts inside the engine with lubricating oil; the oil keeps moving parts from wearing excessively.

The fourth is starting system and its purpose is to change the electrical current into the mechanical energy to push the crankshaft around. By means of this, the engine can be started.

参考译文

汽车发动机是将燃烧热能转化为机械能从而使汽车发动的内燃机。

作为动力来源,发动机需要一个燃料供给系统燃烧空气和燃料的混合物来提供动力。这个系统在动力生产过程中发挥着至关重要的作用。假设发动机是一个汽油机,燃料供给系统从燃油箱中通过燃油泵提供液态汽油进入到化油器,与空气混合。然后混合物被送到发动机燃烧。如果发动机是电喷发动机,燃料则从燃油箱通过电动燃油泵送到喷油器。燃油喷油器通过发动机控制单元脉冲,将直接控制进入进气歧管的制燃油计量。根据发动机状况,发动机控制单元决定发动机的空燃比。

发动机还需要一个制冷系统,因为发动机中空油混合物的燃烧会产生非常高的温度(高达 2 000 ℃到 2 700 ℃)。制冷系统通过液体冷却剂(加了防冻液的水)在发动机和散热器间循环流动为发动机降温,或者通过风冷系统降温。今天,液体制冷发动机是比较普遍的。当制冷剂穿过散热器,温度就会降下来。所以,制冷剂持续在发动机里降温,并有可能会造成一些损害,然后传送到散热器。

发动机还包括润滑系统。润滑系统的目的是为发动机内所有可移动部件提供润滑油;润滑油能够避免可移动部件过度磨损。

第四个系统是发动系统,它的目的是将电流转化成机械能来推动机轴旋转。由此,发动机被发动。

2.3.3 引擎构造

The automobile is designed to travel on roads. The typical automobile has just an internal combustion engine that operates by burning its fuel inside the engine and makes the automobile move. So an engine is the heart of an automobile. See figure 2-59.

A typical automobile engine consists of cylinder block, cylinder head, camshaft, valves, spark plug, piston and piston rings, connecting rod, crankshaft, flywheel and oil pan. See figure 2-60.

Figure 2-59　Engine

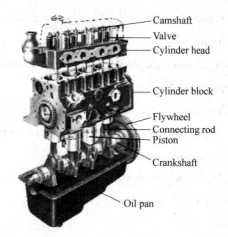

Figure 2-60　Main parts of an engine

Cylinder Block

Cylinder block or engine block, as shown in figure 2-61 and figure 2-62, is a single machined casting unit. It contains the cylinders and the water coolant and lubricant passages. So it is a complicated part at the heart of an engine. Cylinder block is usually made from cast iron or in modern engines, aluminum and magnesium.

Figure 2-61　Inline-engine block

Figure 2-62　V-engine block

Cylinder Head

A cylinder head is a casting generally made from iron or aluminum that holds the valves, spark plugs and one or two camshafts (overhead cam engine only). The cylinder head has machined surfaces to provide a precision fit to mate parts. Inline four-and six-cylinder engines have one cylinder head. V6 and V8 engines have two cylinder heads. The head is essentially a flat plate of metal bolted to the top of the cylinder block with a gasket in between. See figure 2-63 and figure 2-64.

Figure 2-63　Cylinder head (from bottom)

Figure 2-64　Cylinder head (from top)

Camshaft

The key parts of any camshaft are the lobes. As the camshaft spins, the lobes open and close the intake and exhaust valves in time with the motion of the piston. It turns out that there is a direct relationship between the shape of the cam lobes and the way the engine performs in different speed ranges. See figure 2-65 and figure 2-66.

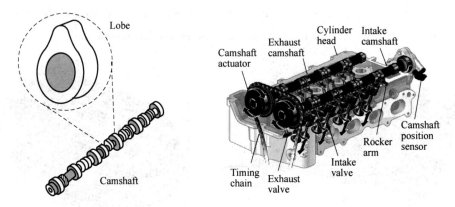

Figure 2-65　Camshaft　　　　　Figure 2-66　Double camshafts

Valves

Valves (figure 2-67 and figure 2-68) are usually made from a steel alloy. Exhaust valves must withstand extremely high temperatures up to 815 degrees Celsius without damaging the valve. The valve face must seat evenly against the valve seat in the cylinder head to prevent leaks from the cylinder during the compression and power strokes. Many valve faces and seats have an angle of 45 degrees.

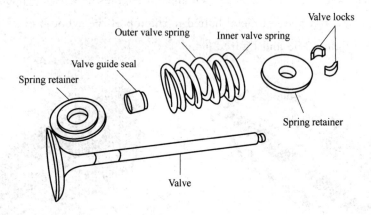

Figure 2-67　Valve assembly

There are intake valves and exhaust valves. On the intake side, the intake valve opens which lets the air-fuel mixture into the combustion chamber. At some point, the intake valve closes, the air-fuel mixture is compressed and ignited by the spark plug. Then the exhaust gas exits the cylinder when the exhaust valve opens (figure 2-68). There are always at least one intake and one exhaust valve. Some cylinder heads have 2 intake and 2 exhaust valves.

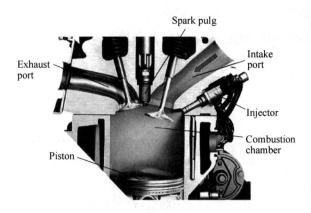

Figure 2-68　Valve

Spark Plug

A spark plug is an electrical device that fits into the cylinder head of some internal combustion engines and ignites compressed air-fuel mixture by means of an electric spark. Spark plugs have an insulated center electrode which is connected by a heavily insulated wire to an ignition coil on the outside. See figure 2-69. The spark plug forces electricity to arc across a gap. The electricity must be at a very high voltage in order to travel across the gap and create a good spark. Voltage at the spark plug can be anywhere from 40 000 to 100 000 volts.

Figure 2-69　Spark plug

New Words and Expressions

combustion [kəmˈbstʃən]　　　　n. 燃烧
cylinder [ˈsilində]　　　　　　　n. 汽缸,圆筒,圆柱体
camshaft [ˈkæmʃæft]　　　　　　n. 凸轮轴
valve [vælv]　　　　　　　　　　n. 阀门,气门
piston [ˈpistən]　　　　　　　　n. 活塞
crankshaft [ˈkræŋkʃæft]　　　　n. 曲轴
flywheel [ˈflaiwi:l]　　　　　　　n. 飞轮
casting [ˈkæstiŋ]　　　　　　　　n. 铸件
contain [kənˈtein]　　　　　　　v. 包含,容纳,含有
coolant [ˈku:lənt]　　　　　　　n. 冷冻剂,冷却液

passage ['pæsidʒ]	n.	通道
complicated ['kɔmplikeitid]	adj.	复杂的
aluminium [ælju'miniəm]	n.	铝
magnesium [mæg'ni:ziəm]	n.	镁
surface ['sə:fis]	n.	表面，平面
precision [pri'siən]	adj.	精确的
mate [meit]	v.	使……配对，使……一致
bolt [bult]	v. 用螺栓连接,用螺栓固定	n. 螺栓
gasket ['gæskit]	n.	衬垫，垫圈
lobe [ləub]	n.	圆突，凸起出部
withstand [wið'stænd]	v.	经得起
device [di'vais]	n.	装置，设备
ignite [ig'nait]	v.	点燃，使燃烧
insulated ['insjuleitid]	adj.	绝缘的
electrode [i'lektrəud]	n.	电极
ignition [ig'niʃən]	n.	点火，着火
voltage ['vəultidʒ]	n.	电压
volt [vɔlt]	n.	伏特

internal combustion engine	内燃机
consists of…	由……组成
cylinder block	汽缸体
cylinder head	汽缸盖
spark plug	火花塞
piston ring	活塞环
oil pan	油底壳
valve spring	气门弹簧
overhead cam engine	顶置凸轮轴发动机
flat plate	平板
connecting rod	连杆
cam lobe	凸轮凸角
intake valve	进气门
exhaust valve	排气门
intake and exhaust valve	进排气门
steel alloy	合金钢
valve seat	气门座
compression stroke	压缩冲程
air-fuel mixture	空气燃油混合气
by means of	用，凭借
insulated wire	绝缘线

ignition coil 点火线圈

Piston and Piston Rings

Piston transforms the energy of the expanding gasses into mechanical energy. They are commonly made of aluminum or cast iron alloys. The piston is a cylindrical shaped hollow part that moves up and down inside the engine cylinder.

Most engine pistons have three rings: the top two are compression rings and the lower ring is oil control ring, and they function as sealing between the piston and the cylinder wall, lubricating, heat transfering and piston supporting in the cylinder. See figure 2-70.

Connection Rod

In a reciprocating piston engine, the connecting rod connects the piston to the crankshaft. In modern internal combustion engines, the connecting rods are most usually made of steel. The small end attaches to the piston pin or wrist pin, which is currently most often press fit into the connecting rod. The big end connects to crankshaft. See figure 2-71.

Figure 2-70 Piston and rings

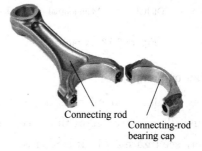
Figure 2-71 Connecting rod

Crankshaft

Crankshafts are made of forged steel. The crankshaft, held in the engine block, converts the reciprocating motion of the pistons into a rotary motion. It provides the turning motion for the wheels. There are usually three journals in a four cylinder engine. To convert the reciprocating motion into rotation, the crankshaft has crankpins, additional bearing surfaces whose axis is offset from that of the crank, to which the "big ends" of the connecting rods attach. The crankshaft has large weights, called counter weights, that balance the weight of the connecting rods. These weights ensure an balance force during the rotation of the moving parts. The crankshaft typically connects to a flywheel, to reduce the vibration caused by the four-stroke cycle. See figure 2-72.

Flywheel

A flywheel is a rotating disc located on one end of the crankshaft and serves three purposes. First, through its inertia, it reduces vibration by smoothing out the power stroke as each cylinder fires. Second, it is mounting surface used to bolt the engine up to its load. Third, the flywheel has gear teeth around its perimeter that allow the starting motor to engage and crank the engine.

The flywheel connected to the crankshaft provides the momentum to keep the crankshaft turning without the application of power, through the energy generated during the power stroke. This energy is also used to drive the crankshaft, connecting rods and pistons during the three idle strokes of the 4-stroke cycle. This makes for a smooth engine speed. The flywheel forms one surface of the clutch and is the base for the ring gear. See figure 2-73.

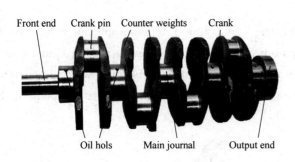

Figure 2-72　Crankshaft　　　　　　　　Figure 2-73　Flywheel

Oil Pan or Sump

Do you wonder what oil pans do? Oil pans are a major engine cooling system parts. They are usually constructed of thin steel and shaped into a deeper section to fully perform its function, see figure 2-74. It is also where the oil pump is placed. When an engine is not running or at rest, oil pans collects the oil as it flows down from the sides of the crankcase. In other words, oil pans that are mounted at the bottom of the crankcase serve as an oil reservoir.

Figure 2-74　Oil Pan

New Words and Expressions

transform [træns'fɔːm]　　　　v. 转换，使……变形
expanding [iks'pændiŋ]　　　　adj. 膨胀的
commonly ['kɔmənli]　　　　　adv. 一般，普通，通常

cylindrical [si'lindrik(ə)l]	adj. 圆柱的
hollow ['hɔləu]	adj. 空的,空腹的,空心的
minimize ['minimaiz]	v. 将……减到最少
friction ['frikʃən]	n. 摩擦,摩擦力
reciprocating [ri'siprəkeitiŋ]	adj. 往复的,来回的
attach [ə'tætʃ]	v. 系上,贴上
convert [kən'və:t]	v. 使转变,使……改变
rotary ['rəutəri]	adj. 旋转的,转动的 n. 运行的机器
rotation [rəu'teiʃən]	n. 旋转,循环
journal ['dvə:nl]	n. 轴颈
crankpin ['kræŋkpin]	n. 曲柄梢
bearing ['bɛəriŋ]	n. 轴承
axis ['æksis]	n. 轴,轴向
offset ['ɔ:fset]	v. 位移,偏移
balance ['bæləns]	n. 平衡 v. 平衡
vibration [vai'breiʃən]	n. 振动
inertia [i'nə:ʃjə]	n. 惯性
perimeter [pə'rimitə]	n. 周长
momentum [məu'mentəm]	n. 动量,冲力,冲量
idle ['aidl]	adj. 懒惰的,停顿的,(机器)空转
lubrication [lu:bri'keiʃən]	n. 润滑
cooling ['ku:liŋ]	n. 冷却 adj. 冷却的
cleaning ['kli:niŋ]	n. 清洁,清洗,净化
mechanical energy	机械能
compression ring	压环
oil ring	油环
cylinder wall	汽缸壁
piston pin / wrist pin	活塞销
press fit	压入配合,压配合
forged steel	锻钢
forged iron	锻铁
rotary motion	旋转运动
smooth out	弄平(消除)
reciprocating motion	往复运动
counter weights	平衡重
four-stroke cycle	四冲程工作循环
ring gear	齿圈
oil reservoir	机油罐

Figure 2-75 is the automobile engine, and table 2-2 is engine parts.

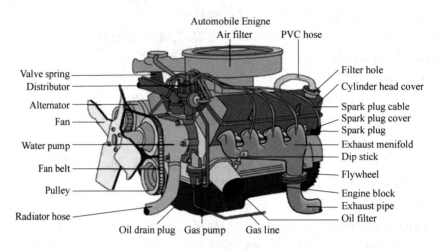

Figure 2-75 Automobile engine

Table 2-2 Engine parts

English Terms	Explanations	Chinese
Valve spring	Mechanism that keeps the valve closed	气门弹簧
Distributor	Case that enables engine's ignition	分电器
Alternator	Generator that enables current in both directions	交流发电机
Fan	Apparatus that feed oxygen into the engine's combustion	风扇
Water pump	Device that circulates water through the radiator	水泵
Fan belt	Piece of rubber that wraps around the pulleys and turns the cooling fan	风扇皮带
Pulley	Small wheel with a grooved rim, bitted with a belt, which turns the cooling fan	带轮
Radiator hose	Treated rubber tube that connects the lines of a combustion engine	散热器软管
fuel pump	Device that moves gas from the gas tank to the engine	燃油泵
fuel line	Network of hoses that transport the gas	燃油管路
Air filter	Device that removes impurities from air passing through it	空气滤清器
Dip stick	Instrument that measures the level of oil in a motor	机油量尺
Engine block	Set consisting the motor, the clutch and the gearbox	发动机气缸体
Cylinder head cover	Removable cover on the upper part of the motor	汽缸盖罩盖
Spark plug cable	Cable connecting the spark plug to the distributor cap	火花塞高压线
Spark plug	Ignition device of an internal combustion engine	火花塞
Exhaust manifold	System that collects spent gases	排气歧管
Flywheel	Wheel that regulates the speed of the engine while turning	飞轮
Exhaust pipe	Pipe through which spent gas is expelled	排气管
Oil filter	Device that removes impurities from oil passing through it	机油滤清器

2.4 保 养

2.4.1 保养的类型和周期

Maintenance is nothing more than cleaning and washing, trouble shooting, mounting-part tightening, lubricating, filling, adjusting and other operations which are carried out, as a rule, without disassembling parts and taking them down.

汽车保养不外乎指车辆清洁和清洗,故障排除、零部件紧固、润滑、填充、调整以及其他工序这些操作,这些操作通常是在不拆卸零件并取下的情况下进行的。

Regulations divide maintenance into a number of types depending on their recurrence, scope of work and labour requirements involved in each particular case. These types are: daily maintenance, level 1 maintenance, level 2 maintenance and seasonal maintenance.

根据保养周期、工作范围,以及特殊车况所用工时,汽车保养可以分为:日常保养、一级保养、二级保养和季节性保养。

Daily maintenance consists of cleaning and washing operations and checking the overall condition of the car so as to ensure its safe operation and appropriate appearance. The car is cleaned and washed, inspected, filled with fuel, oil and coolant. Daily maintenance is timed with the beginning or end of a shift.

日常保养包括清洁、清洗工作和检查整车工况以确保汽车安全运行和外表整洁。清洁、清洗、检查汽车并加注燃料、机油和冷却剂。日常保养定期在出车前或收车后。

Level 1 maintenance calls for the repeating of all daily maintenance operations followed by a number of additional operations involving the tightening of mounting parts, lubricating, inspecting and adjusting of units and parts which are all carried out without dismounting and disassembling them.

一级保养在重复所有日常保养后还要进行若干其他附加工作,包括零部件紧固、润滑、检查以及调整汽车装置和部件,无须拆卸。

Level 2 maintenance stipulates a repetition of level 1 maintenance in the wake of which more inspections and adjustments follow which are extended in scope and require partial disassembling of units. Some of them are taken down from the car and tested on the test stands.

二级保养规定在重复一级保养工作后扩大范围进行更多的检查和调整,需要拆卸部分装置。其中一些部件从汽车上拆下,然后放到试验台上进行检验。

Seasonal maintenance is timed to be carried out twice a year, and involved in this case are operations associated with the seasonal changeover. Seasonal maintenance often coincides with level 2 maintenance. Specified for seasonal maintenance are commonly the following operations: washing the cooling system, changing the lubricant in the engine crankcase and in the oil baths of other units (fresh oil of a grade appropriate for the coming season should be used), checking the fuel system and washing the fuel tank. The cold-starting aid and the cab heater are tested for performance at the beginning of operation.

季节性保养一年两次，保养工作跟季节转换相关。季节性保养经常与二级保养同步进行。季节保养的特有操作通常包括：清洗冷却系统、更换发动机曲轴箱润滑油和其他装置油槽的机油（应该使用适合下个季节的新油）、检查燃油系统和清洗燃油箱。操作从对冷启动辅助装置和驾驶室加热器进行性能测试开始。

The recurrence of maintenance is decided by the kilometers logged by every car under given service conditions.

汽车保养周期根据每辆车在特定行驶状况下的行驶里程数而定。

2.4.2 车辆保养中的诊断

Diagnostics of various kinds of cars aimed at assessing the technical condition of vehicles finds wide-spread application at garages. It is a systematic checkup of a vehicle's performance without taking its units apart, which is carried out with the aid of special equipment and furnishes unbiased evidence of the vehicle's fitness for further service. Distinction is made between general diagnostics and piecemeal diagnostics.

对不同种类的车辆进行诊断在修理厂得到广泛应用，旨在判断汽车的技术状况。这是对汽车性能进行的系统性检查，无须拆卸零部件，检查时借助专门的设备并出具车况完好的证据以保证该车可以继续使用。总体诊断和零星诊断是有区别的。

The former serves to assess the condition of the units which are critical from the standpoint of safe driving. The latter is intended to gauge the condition of the units with the aim of finding out the causes of various troubles and determine the scope of maintenance and repair work to be done.

前者评估车辆状况，这从安全驾驶角度来讲至关重要。后者评定部件状况是为了查出各种故障的原因，确定要做的保养和维修工作的范围。

New Words and Expressions

maintenance ['meintinəns]　　　　　　 n. 维护，保持，维修
tightening ['taitniŋ]　　　　　　　　　 n. 上紧，固定
lubricating ['luːbrikeitiŋ]　　　　　　 n. 润滑，涂油
adjusting [əˈdvʌstiŋ]　　　　　　　　 n. 调整，校正
disassemble [disəˈsembl]　　　　　　 v. 拆卸
regulation [regjuˈleiʃən]　　　　　　 n. 规则，规章
recurrence [riˈkʌrəns]　　　　　　　 n. 再现，循环
scope [skəup]　　　　　　　　　　　 n. 范围
appropriate [əˈprouprieIt]　　　　　 adj. 合适的，恰当的
overall [ˈəuvərɔːl]　　　　　　　　　 adj. 综合的，全面的
inspect [inˈspekt]　　　　　　　　　 v. 检查，调查

coolant ['ku:lənt]	n.	冷却剂
inspection [in'spekʃən]	n.	检查,视察
dismounting [dis'mauntiŋ]	n.	拆卸,拆散,拆除
stipulate ['stipjuleit]	v.	规定,明定
repetition [repi'tiʃən]	n.	重复,反复
changeover ['tʃeindʒ'əuvə]	n.	转换,逆转
lubricant ['lu:brikənt]	adj.	润滑的
crankcase ['kræŋkkeis]	n.	曲轴箱
cab [kæb]	n.	驾驶室
diagnostics [ˌdaɪəgˈnɑːstɪkz]	n.	诊断学
garage [gə'rɑ:ʒ]	n.	车库,修理厂
unbiased [ʌn'baɪəst]	adj.	公正的,不偏不倚的,无偏见的
assess [ə'ses]	v.	评估
gauge [geɪdʒ]	v.	判定,判断,估计
be nothing more than		只不过是
mounting part		固定件,装配件
in the wake of		紧随其后
test stand		试验台
be associated with		与……有关,与……有关系
oil bath		油槽

2.4.3 调回汽车里程表数值

A blonde made several attempts to sell her old car. She was having a lot of problems finding a buyer because the car had 340 000 miles on it. She discussed her problems with a brunette that she worked with at a bar.

The brunette suggested:"There may be a chance to sell that car more easily, but it's not going to be legal."

"That doesn't matter at all", replied the blonde, "all that matter is that I am able to sell this car."

"Alright", replied the brunette. In a quiet voice, she told the blonde:"Here is the address of a friend of mine. He owns a car repair shop around here. Tell him I sent you, and he will turn the counter back on your car to 40 000 miles. Then it shouldn't be a problem to sell your car."

The following weekend, the blonde took a trip to mechanic on the brunette's advice.

About one month after that, the brunette saw the blonde and asked, "Did you sell your car?"

"No," replied the blonde. "Why should I? It only has 40 000 miles on it."

一位金发女郎多次尝试卖掉她的旧车,但是很难找到买家,因为她的汽车里程表显示这辆车已经行驶了34万英里。于是她向一位一起在酒吧里工作的黑发女郎讲了她的问题。

黑发女郎说:"我有一个方法可以让你很容易就卖掉你的车,但是这样做会违法。"

金发女郎回答道:"没关系,只要能卖掉车,什么方法都无所谓。"

黑发女郎接着说:"好吧。"然后悄悄地告诉金发女郎:"这是我一个朋友的地址,他在这附近开了一家汽车维修店。告诉他是我介绍你去的,他会把你车上的计数器调到4万英里。这样你把车卖掉就没有问题了。"

第二周周末,金发女郎按照黑发女郎的建议去了那家维修店。

大约一个月后,黑发女郎见到了金发女郎,便问道:"你的车卖掉了吗?"

金发女郎回答说:"没有,我为什么要卖掉它,里程表上只有4万英里。"

2.5 汽车市场

2.5.1 怎样变成一个好的汽车销售?

Selling cars is a good career fit for many people. As with many professions, selling cars involves a combination of talent, people skills, and aptitude. If you think you have that kind of personality, you can do a few things to prepare yourself for success.

Instructions:

Assess your sales skills. It's important to have the ability to listen and pick up on subtle verbal cues, as well as observe body language.

Observe the sales techniques and approaches of other salespeople.

Ask questions that require something more than a one-word response. The more you can draw out a customer about what he really wants in a car, the easier it will be to persuade her to accept the makes and models you recommend.

Understand the financial limits of your client. If the individual mentions she can afford to spend only a certain amount of money, use that as your starting point. Taking her at her word and beginning in the range she mentions will help strengthen the connections between salesman and customer, who may willingly concede to being able to afford to pay a little more.

Know your inventory thoroughly. It is necessary to be familiar with each make and model, current level of quality, and price of vehicles on the lot. Being able to quickly match a customer with one or more options in vehicles will increase the chances of making a sale.

Look for the right opportunity to close the deal. The right word or the mention of an added benefit will usually move the customer from looking around to making a commitment.

如何成为一名优秀的汽车销售员

汽车销售是一种很多人都适合的职业。和许多行业一样,汽车销售工业要求天赋、人际交往能力和才能的综合。如果你认为你有这样的能力,你就可以开始行动,做好走向成功的准备。

指导原则：

评估你的销售技巧。具备倾听，能够捕捉微妙语言信号以及观察细微肢体语言的能力很重要。

观察揣摩其他销售人员的销售技巧和方法。

问顾客一些需要用较多的话语而不是一个字来回答的问题。你对顾客的真正购车需求了解得越多，就越容易促使她接受你推荐的品牌和型号。

了解客户的财力限额。如果她提到她只花得起一定数额的钱，那么就把这个数额作为向她推销的起点。相信她所说的，并在她提到的范围内开始推销将有助于加强客户与销售人员之间的联系。客户可能会愿意做出让步，出价更高一些。

清楚地了解库存情况。你需要熟悉每一款汽车的品牌和型号，以及它们的质量和当前价格水平。能够快速地把顾客要求与一种或更多的汽车款式联系起来，将增加成功售出汽车的机会。

寻找合适的机会完成交易。恰当的话语或提及附加的好处通常会使顾客从物色转向做出决定。

2.5.2 对话练习

Directions: Work in pairs. Practice the following dialogue about car logos.

Salesman: Can I help you, madam?

Customer: I'd like an AUDI A8 2.0T with a sunroof and leather seats.

Salesman: All right, there are 5 colors for you to choose from. They are black, white, red, silver and blue.

Customer: I like the black one.

Salesman: OK. I'll prepare a set of contracts. Before signing them, I need your credit card for authorization.

Customer: Wait a moment, please. What's the price?

Salesman: 500 000 Yuan in total, including tax, interest for 60 months, and a 50 000 down payment.

Customer: Oh, that's too expensive. How about 400 000? Is that workable?

Salesman: No, I'm afraid not. If we do it this way, the down payment has to be 50%.

Customer: OK. I'll take one if you offer some kind of discount.

Salesman: Well, 8 000 lower is our final offer.

Customer: All right, it's a deal.

第 3 章　电子信息专业英语

3.1　电子信息专业英语基础知识

1. 合成词

multimeter：万用表

interface：接口，界面

code-decode →codec：编解码

coder-decoder →codec：编解码器

modulator-demolator→modem：调制解调器

Interactive-network → internet：互联网，因特网

transmitter-receiver → transceiver：收发器

electronic 电子的：electronic mail(Email)

electric 电的：electric voltage 电压；electric current 电流；electric resistance 电阻

electrical 电气的：electric engineer 电气工程师；electric property 电性能

electro- 电-：electromagnetic wave 电磁波；electrodynamic 电动的

electrode：电极

anode：阳极，正极

cathode：阴极，负极

positive：阳性的，正的，正数

negative：阴性的，负的，负数

2. 专业词汇

diode：二极管

triode：三极(真空)管

transistor：晶体管，三极管

field-effect transistor：场效应晶体管(FET)

amplifier：放大器

Ohm's Law：欧姆定律

oscillator:振荡器
oscilloscope:示波器
radio:无线电、收音机
radar:雷达
laser:激光
machine language:机器语言
assembler/assembly language:汇编语言
high-level language:高级语言

3．转意词汇

resistance→阻力，抵抗，敌对→电阻(值)
current→水流，气流，趋势，当前的→电流
charge→装载，起诉，负责，载荷→电荷，充电
circuit→周围，巡回，绕行→电路
power→力量，动力→电源，功率，动力，电力，幂
field→田野，场地，领域→(电、磁)场
bus→公共汽车→总线
network→网、网状组织→网络
rectifier→修正者→整流器
regulator→调整者→稳压器
Monitor→班长→显示器，监视器

resistance：电阻,电阻值　　resistor：电阻(器)
capacitance：电容,电容值　　capacitor：电容(器)
inductance：电感,电感值　　inductor：电感(器)
differential：微分　　　　　difference：差分
probability：概率　　　　　possibility：可能性
parallel(serial)：并行(串行)
parallel(series)：并联(串联)
analog(digital)：模拟的(数字的)
continuous(discrete)：连续的(离散的)

4．专业缩写词

FET(field-effect transistor):场效应管
IC(integrated circuit):集成电路
USB(universal serial bus):通用串行总线
AM(amplitude modulation):幅度调制,调幅
FM(frequency modulation):频率调制,调频
DC．dc．(direct current):直流
AC．ac．(alternating current):交流
LAN(local area network):局域网

MAN(metropolitan area network):城域网
WAN(wide area network):广域网
WWW(world wide web):全球网,万维网
HTTP(hypertext transfer protocol):超文本传送协议
GPRS(general packet radio service):通用无线分组业务
ASCII(American Standard Code for Information Interchange):美国信息交换标准码
ISDN(integrated services digital network):综合业务数字网
FFT(fast fourier transform):快速傅里叶变换
IFFT(inverse fast fourier transform):逆快速傅里叶变换
CRT(cathode ray tube):阴极射线管(显示器)
(Chinese Remainder Theorem):中国剩余定理
ATM (automatic teller machine):自动取款机
　　　(asynchronous transfer mode):异步转移(传递)模式

5. 机构的缩写

ITU(International Telecommunications Union):国际电信联盟
IEEE(Institute of Electrical and Electronics Engineering):电气与电子工程师协会
ISO(International Standardization Organization):国际标准化组织
IEC(International Electro technical Commission):国际电工委员会
ANSI(American National Standards Institute):美国国家标准学会
AT&T(American Telephone & Telegraph):美国电话电报公司

6. 数制

binary　　二进制　　　　octal　　八进制
decimal　　十进制　　　　hexadecimal 十六进制

Table 3-1　十进制表

		10^0	10^1	10^2	10^3	10^4	10^5	10^6	10^7	10^8	10^9	10^{10}	10^{11}	10^{12}	10^{13}	10^{14}	10^{15}	10^{16}	10^{17}	10^{18}
汉语	大		个	十	百	千		万				亿				兆				京
	小	个	十	百	千	万	亿	兆	京	垓										
英美	美	unit	ten	hundred	thousand			million			billion			trillion			quadrillion			
	英	unit	ten	hundred	thousand			million						billion						trillion

Table 3-1 为十进制表。

7. 国际单位制

Table 3-2 国际单位(部分)

量	单位	单位符号
length	meter	m
mass	kilogram	kg
time	second	s
angle	radian	rad
electric current	ampere	A
electric capacitance	farad	F
electric charge	coulomb	C
electric potential	volt	V
electric resistance		Ω
electric frequency	hertz	Hz
electric inductance	henry	H
electric power	watt	W
thermodynamic	Kelvin degree	K
temperature	Celsius degree	℃

Table 3-2 所示为部分国际单位。

8. 电子信息专业英语中的常见表达

(1) 以……为单位

in units of……; in……

例:an angle in radians

current in amperes

where f is in hertz and v is in volts

in thousands

in billions of dollars

注意单位名用复数形式。

(2) A 的大小/数量/重量/……是 B 的 N 倍;A 比 B 大/多/重/…… $N-1$ 倍

A is N times as large/many/heavy/ … as B

A is N times larger/more/heavier / … as B

A is larger/more/heavier / … than B by N times

(3) 增加到二倍/三倍/四倍/五倍……

A double /treble/quadruple/quintuple …

例:We double the voltage.

(4) 增加为 N 倍,或增加了 $N-1$ 倍

increase to N times

increase by N times

increase by a factor of N

increase N-fold

increase N times as much/many/… as

例：increase by $x\%$

(5) 减少了$(N-1)/N$倍,或减少到$1/N$

reduce by $x\%$

decrease N times

decrease to N times

decrease by N times

decrease by a factor of N

decrease N-fold

decrease N times as much/many/… as

N-fold reduction/decrease

be N times less than

例1：The switching time of the new type transistor is shortened by a third.
新型晶体管的开关时间缩短为三分之一 。

例2：The cost of TV sets was reduced by 70％.
电视机的成本降低了70％。

例3：The voltage has dropped four-fifths.
电压下降了五分之四 。

例4：The maximum communication rate in this network is 64 kbit/s.
该网络中的最大通信速率为64 kbit/s。

例5：The upper working temperature limit of this machine is 45 ℃.
本机最高工作温度为45 ℃。

9. 图

(1) 图的编号

对于较短的文章,可将所有图按顺序统一编号。例如：

① Figure 1 , Figure 2 , …

② Fig. 1 , Fig. 2 , …

对于较长的文章,可将所有图分章节编号。例如：

① Figure 1-1, Figure1-2, …, Figure 2-1, Figure 2-2 …

② Fig. 1-1, Fig. 1-2, …, Fig. 2-1, Fig. 2-2 …

(2) 图的来源

如果图是自己创作的,可不作说明,如果是引自其他文献,则有必要在图旁或题后注明来源。例如：

Fig. 1 the AT&T telephone hierarchy.

(Source：Andrew S. Tandenbaum. Computer Networks)

(3) 与图有关的词或词组

block diagram	方框图
schematic diagram	示意图/原理图

circuit diagram	电路图/线路图
connection diagram	连接图/接线图
wiring diagram	布线图
phase diagram	相位图
state diagram	状态图
signal state diagram	信号状态图
Venn diagram	维恩图/文氏图
line graph	线图
curve line graph	曲线图
broken line graph	折线图
bar graph	条形图
statistical chart/diagram	统计图表
flow chart	流程图
diagrammatic sketch	示意图/略图
vectogram	矢量图/向量图
histogram	直方图/柱状图

(4) 与图有关的表达用语

① Something may be described by the block diagram shown in figure 1-1.

② Figure 6-1 illustrates the relationship among A，B and C.

③ The scanning procedure is illustrated in figure 2-1.

④ Figure 14-1 shows a simplified block diagram of something.

⑤ In the analog world，images are usually presented as horizontal raster lines（see figure 14-2）.

⑥ In figure 2-2，…

⑦ As the figure shows，…

⑧ …，as illustrated in figure 2-2.

10. 表

(1) 表的编号

表的编号类似于图的编号,例如：

① Table 1，Table 2 ，…

② Tab.1，Tab.2 ，…

③ Table 1-1，Table 1-2，…

④ Tab. 1-1，Tab. 1-2，…

(2) 表的来源

表的来源类似于图的来源,例如：

Tab.1 A comparison of semiconductor diodes and LEDs as light sources.

(Source：Andrew S. Tandenbaum. Computer Networks)

3.2 翻译准则

翻译的准则

(1) 信 True；(2) 达 Smooth；(3) 雅 Refined.

例 1：Because computers are binary machines, the program stored in a computer's main memory must be in binary form. Few programmers actually write machine-level instructions, however.

因为计算机是二进制的机器,存储在计算机主存储器里的程序必须是二进制形式的。然而,实际上极少程序员使用机器级的指令。

例 2：In the AND circuit, "1" signals on all inputs give a "1" output; output is "0", if all inputs are not "1".

在"与"电路中,若所有输入端为"1"信号,则输出"1"；若输入端不全为"1",则输出"0"。

例 3：As rubber prevents electricity from passing through it, it is used as insulating material.

因为橡胶不导电,所以用作绝缘材料。

例 4：In computer we use bit to represent the minimum data.

在计算机中我们用位来表示最小的数据。

例 5：The miniature receiving antenna was developed as an alternative to that large one.

这种小型接收天线是为取代那种大型天线而研制的。

例 6：Gases differ from solids in that the former have greater compressibility than the latter.

气体与固体的区别在于前者较后者有更大的可压缩性。

例 7：Reliability features this control system.

可靠性是这个控制系统的特色。

例 8：Integrated circuits were successfully developed in American in 1958.

集成电路于1958年在美国研制成功。

例 9：An electric field can be produced by any charges present in space.

空间存在的任何电荷均会产生电场。

例 10：Any substance is made of atoms, whether it is a gas, a liquid, or a solid.

任何物质,无论是气体、液体或固体,皆由原子组成。

例 11：It is thirty cubic meters in volume.

体积是30立方米。

例 12：The first term of Fourier series is called the fundamental, the others is called the harmonics.

傅里叶级数的第一项称为基波,其他各项称为谐波。

例 13：The attenuation of the filter is nearly constant to within 0.5 dB over the entire frequency band.

该滤波器的衰减近于恒定，整个频带内的变化在 0.5 dB 以内。

例 14：The product yield is a sensitive function of process control.

产品的成品率与工艺控制密切相关。

3.3　电子信息专业英语阅读材料

Resistors：A resistor is an electrical component that resists the flow of electrical current. The amount of current （I） flowing in a circuit is directly proportional to the voltage across it and inversely proportional to the resistance of the circuit. This is Ohm's law and can be expressed as a formula：$I=UR/R$. The resistor is generally a linear device and its characteristics form a straight line when plotted on a graph.

电阻器：电阻器是一种能阻碍电流流动的电子器件。电阻器中流过的电流（I）与加在电阻两端的电压成正比，与电阻的阻值成反比。这就是欧姆定律，可以用公式表示成 $I=UR/R$。电阻器通常是线性器件，它的（伏安）特性曲线是一条直线。

Resistors are used to limit current flowing to a device, thereby preventing it from burning out, as voltage dividers to reduce voltage for other circuits, as transistor biasing circuits, and to serve as circuit loads.

电阻器常用作限流器，以限制流过器件的电流，以防止器件因流过的电流过大而烧坏。电阻器也可以用作分压器，以减小其他电路的电压，如晶体管偏置电路。电阻器还可用作电路的负载。

Generally, resistors （figure 3-1） consist of carbon composition, wire-wound, and metal film. The size of resistors depends on power ratings. Larger sizes are referred to as power resistors. Variable resistors are adjustable：rheostats, potentiometers, and trimmer pots. Precision resistors have a tolerance of 1% or less.

一般来说，电阻有碳（膜）电阻、线绕电阻和金属膜电阻（如 Figure 3-1 所示），电阻器尺寸的大小与电阻的（额定）功率有关，尺寸比较大的电阻器通常是高功率电阻器。可变电阻器是电阻值可调节的电阻器，如变阻器、电位器和微调电位器。精密电阻器是指其误差率在 1% 或更小的电阻器。

If you are a bit serious about the electronics hobby I recommend learning the "Color Code". It makes a lot easier. The same color code is used for everything else, like coils, capacitors etc. Again, just the color code associated with a number, like：black＝0, brown＝1 red＝2, etc. Figure 3-2 is an example; it is a 4-band resistor.

如果你对电子技术颇有兴趣，建议学会电阻的"彩色条形码"识别方法，这样会带来很多方便。而且这种彩色条形码标注方法在其他器件上也适用，如线圈（电感）、电容等。这种方法是用色彩表示数字，如黑色＝0，棕色＝1，红色＝2 等。Figure 3-2 是个彩色条形码电阻的例子。

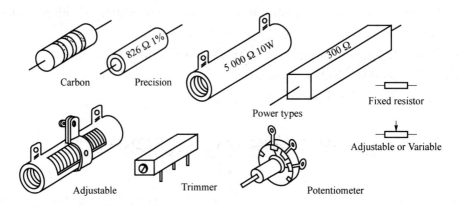

Figure 3-1 Various Resistors

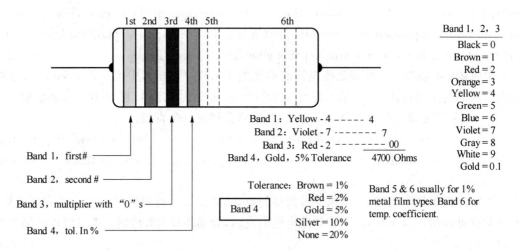

Figure 3-2 An example of resistor color code

Can you "create" your own resistors? Of cause and not difficult. Here is how to do it. Draw a line on a piece of paper with a soft pencil, HB or 2B will do fine. Make the line thick and about 2 inches (5 cm) long. With your multimeter, measure the Ohm's value of this line by putting a probe on each side of the line, make sure the probes are touching the carbon from the pencil. The value would probably be around the 800 kΩ to 1.5 MΩ depending line. The resistance will drop considerably, if you erase some of it (length-wise obviously!). You can also use carbon with silicon glue and when it dries measure the resistance, etc.

自己可以制作一个电阻(器)吗？当然可以,而且也不难。这里教你如何做一个电阻(器),用一支软铅笔(HB 铅笔或用 2B 铅笔更好),在纸上画一段大约 2 英寸(5 cm)长的粗线。用万用表测量这段线的欧姆值,(方法是)把万用表的两支探笔分别与铅笔线的两端相接触,一定要让探笔与线端的碳接触。根据线的粗细,电阻值大约为 800 kΩ～1.5 MΩ。如果你擦掉一些线,使线明显变短,电阻值就会变小。你也可以用掺有硅胶的碳粉来制作电阻器,当硅胶干了以后测量其电阻值等。

Capacitors: A capacitor is an electrical device that can temporarily store electrical energy. Basically, a capacitor consists of two conductors (metal plates) separated by a dielectric insulating material [figure 3-3(a)], which increases the ability to store a charge.

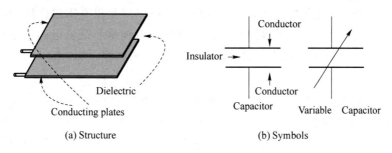

Figure 3-3　Capacitor

电容器:电容器是可以暂时存储电能的电子器件。电容器一般由两块导体(金属极板)组成[见 Figure 3-3(a)],中间用一层不导电的绝缘材料隔开,这层绝缘材料可以增加电容存储电荷的本领(即增大电容量)。

The dielectric can be paper, plastic film, mica, ceramic, air or a vacuum. The plates can be aluminum discs, aluminum foil or a thin film of metal applied to opposite sides of a solid dielectric. The conductor-dielectric-conductor sandwich can be rolled into a cylinder or left flat, the symbols of capacitor are shown in figure 3-3(b).

绝缘材料可以是纸、塑料片、云母、陶瓷材料、空气或真空。极板可以是薄铝板、铝箔或在一片两面各贴上一层金属薄膜的绝缘板。可以直接把一个这种导体-绝缘体-导体(三明治式)制成平板电容器,也可以把它卷起来成为圆柱形电容器。电容器的符号如 Figure 3-3(b)所示。

A capacitor will block DC current, but appears to pass AC current by charging and discharging. It develops an AC resistance, known as capacitive reactance, which is affected by the capacitance and AC frequency. The formula for capacitive reactance is $X_C = 1/(2fC)$, with units of ohms.

电容器隔直流电,但能以充电和放电的方式通过交流电。它构成的交流电阻抗称为容抗。容抗与电容量和交流电的频率有关,容抗的公式为 $X_C=1/(2\pi fC)$,其单位为欧姆。

Inductors: An inductor is an electrical device, which can temporarily store electromagnetic energy in the field about it as long as current is flowing through it. The inductor is a coil of wire that may have an air core or an iron core to increase its inductance. A powered iron core in the shape of a cylinder may be adjusted in and out of the core.

电感器:当电流流过电感器时,电感器周围就有电磁场,电感器是以电磁场的形式暂时存储电磁能量的电子器件。电感器是一组线圈,有的电感器线圈中有可增加其电感量的铁芯,可调电感有一个强磁的圆柱状铁芯,通过调节铁芯可以增加或减少电感量。

An inductor tends to oppose a change in electrical current, it has no resistance to DC current but has an AC resistance to AC current, known as inductive reactance, this inductive reactance is affected by inductance and the AC frequency and is given by the formula $X_L = 2fL$, with units of ohms. Inductors are used for filtering AC current, increasing the output of the RF (radio frequency) amplifier.

电感器有阻碍电流变化的趋势,对直流电而言,电感器是没有阻碍作用的,但对交流电来说,电感器有一个交流阻抗,称为感抗。这个感抗与电感量和交流电的频率有关,可以用公式表示为 $X_L = 2\pi fL$,其单位为欧姆。电感器可以用来滤波、增加 RF(无线电频率)放大器的输出。

Inductors are available in variety of shapes (figure 3-4): air core, iron core (which may look like a transformer, but has only two leads), toroidal (doughnut shaped), small tubular with epoxy, RF choke with separate coils on a cylinder, and tunable RF coil with a screwdriver adjustment.

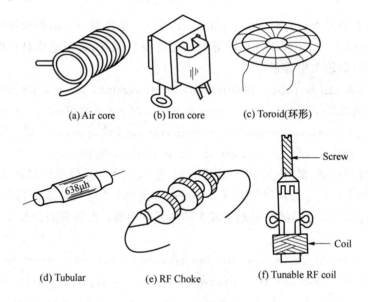

Figure 3-4 Various inductors

电感器有各式各样的形状(如 Figure 3-4 所示),空芯的、铁芯的(铁芯的有时看起来像个变压器,但只有两个端口)、环状的(圆环形的)、管状的(以环氧树脂为材料)、RF 扼流圈是由圆柱上分开的线圈构成,而且可调的线圈带有一把调整螺丝刀。

New Words and Expressions

reactance	n. 电抗
resistance	n. 电阻值,中文有时简称电阻
resistor	n. 电阻器,中文有时简称电阻
voltage	n. 电压,伏特数
capacitance	n. 电容量
capacitor	n. 电容器
charge	n. 负荷,电荷,充电 v. 装满,充电
dielectric	n. 电介质,绝缘体 adj. 非传导性的
electrical	adj. 电的,有关电的

formula	*n.*	公式,规则,客套话
inductance	*n.*	电感量,电感值
inductor	*n.*	诱导物,感应器,电感器
insulating	*adj.*	绝缘的
multimeter	*n.* 万用表 *vt.*	多点测量
probe	*n.*	探针,外太空探测器

be inversely proportional to 与……成反比
be affected by… 受……影响
be available 是可利用的,可用的
be directly proportional to… 与……成正比
be expressed as… 被表示成……
be proportional to… 与……成比例
be used to… 被用于……
in various shapes and sizes 各种形状和尺寸
to serve as… 用作……

第4章　城市轨道交通专业英语

4.1　问路和指路

4.1.1　常用问路指路的句式

Asking the way and giving directions are very important during our daily life. If you are new comer you may get lost, you need to ask the way from police or local people. There are many ways to ask. "Excuse me, could you tell me the way to …?" "Hello, how can I get to …" "Excuse me, is there a … near here?" Of course you should know the directions. "Go straight ahead till you see a traffic light. Then turn left. It is on the right side of the road. It's opposite to a big shopping mall. You can't miss it."

Meanwhile when we ask the way or give directions, we should be polite to others. Most of the time we use "Excuse me" "Please…" or "Could you…" You should remember that!

1. Asking the way 问路

Excuse me, can you tell me the way to…

Excuse me, would you please tell me how I can get …

Can you show me the way to …

Is there a bank near here?

2. Giving directions 指路

Go along the street.

Turn right at the first crossing.

Turn left at the second traffic light.

You can take subway line 4, and interchange at Chongwenmen Station. Then take subway line 2, and get off at Beijing Station.

It's about 5 minute's walk.

4.1.2 各种问路指路情景对话

Dialogue 1

某人要从三坝附近到杭州火车东站去。

P:Passenger(乘客)　　　M:Metro Staff(地铁工作人员)

P:Excuse me, how can I get to the Hangzhoudong Railway Station?

打扰了,我怎样才能去杭州火车东站?

M:You can't get there directly from here. You should get off at Fengqi Road Station and transfer to line 1.

从这里不能直接去火车东站。您必须在风起路站下车,换乘1号线。

P:Could you put it more precisely?

您能说得详细点吗?

M:Sure! When you get off at Fengqi Road Station, you should walk for 5 minutes (about 300 meters) and then arrive at the platform of line 1 towards the direction of Xiashajiangbin, take 5 stops to East Railway Station.

当然!您在凤起路下车,走5分钟(约300米)然后到达1号线往下沙江滨方向的站台,换乘1号线,坐5站到达火车东站。

P:Which exit should I take?

我到了之后该从哪个出口出去呢?

M:Exit D is right.

到了之后在D出口出。

P:Thank you very much!

非常感谢!

M:You are welcome!

不客气!

Dialogue 2

某人要从三坝附近到杭州火车站。

P: Excuse me, Miss?

M: Yes? Is there anything I can do for you?

P: I want to go to the Hangzhou Railway Station. Can you tell me how to get there?

M: Sure. You can take subway line 2, get on the train at Sanba Station and get off at Fengqi Road Station which is a transfer station, change to line 1 and get off at Chengzhan Station. You cannot miss it.

P: I beg your pardon? Which station shall I get off to change another line?

M: Chengzhan Station.

P: Ok, thank you very much.

M: You're welcome. Have a nice journey.

P: Thanks, bye.

Dialogue 3

某人从杨家墩拉喜美食街要到西湖去。

P:Excuse me, how can I get to the West Lake?

打扰了,请问到西湖怎么走?

M:First, you can walk to Yangjiadun Subway Station, Second, you can take line 4 to Jinjiang Station, then, change to line 1 and get off at Fengqi Road Station.

先步行到杨家墩地铁站,然后乘4号线到近江站,到了那里再换乘1号线到凤起路下车。

P:How long did it take to get there?

到那里要花多长时间?

M:About an hour.

大约一小时。

P:Okay. Could you tell me the last trains running schedule of Fengqi Road Station and Jinjiang Station? I'm afraid of missing it.

好的。您能告诉我凤起路站和近江站的末班车时间吗? 我怕错过时间。

M:Please wait a moment and let me have a check. The last subway on line 4 to Pengbu direction passes Jinjiang Station at 22:58, while line 1 to Xiashajiangbin direction is at 22:53. So you'd better get to Jinjiang Station earlier.

请等一下,我查查。4号线往彭埠方向的末班车是22:58经过近江站,但1号线往下沙江滨方向的末班车是22:53。您最好早点赶到近江站。

P:I see. Many thanks for helping here!

我知道了。非常感谢您的帮助!

M:You're welcome.

不客气。

Dialogue 4

P:Excuse me, where am I in this map?

请问我现在在地图上哪个位置?

M:You are here, Citizen Center Station, the subway station, in the heart of the city.

您现在在这里,市民中心站。城市中心位置下的地铁站。

P:Oh, I think I am lost. Can I go from here to Hangzhou Olympic Sports Center?

我想我迷路了。我从这里能到杭州奥体中心吗?

M:Sure! You can walk 300 meters from the exit F to the Citizen Center bus station, and then take NO.96 bus to the Hangzhou Olympic Sports Center station.

您可以从F口出去走300米到达市民中心公交站,然后坐96路公交车到杭州奥体中心。

Dialogue 5

P:Excuse me, could you tell me how to get to Wulinmen Station from here by subway? This is my first time to take subway.

打扰了,您能告诉我从这儿怎样乘坐地铁去武林门么？这是我第一次乘坐地铁。

M:Sure! First ,you should buy a passenger ticket,scan the ticket on entrance gate so as to cross it. Then,you can go downstairs and take the train on the platform.

当然可以,首先您需要买张票,把票放在闸机上刷一下,然后下楼去站台乘车。

P:How long will it take to get there?

到那里要多久?

M:You'd better take line 1 train bound for Chaoyang Station at this station. After 7 stations,you will arrive at your destination for about 31 minutes. If you take line 5, it would be wrong.

您在本站坐2号线到杭州东火车站方向的列车,只要7站,需要31分钟。如果您乘坐5号线就坐错了。

P:I see. By the way,how can I walk out of the platform after getting off the train?

我明白了,顺便问一下,我下车后怎么从站台出去呢?

M:That's easy. Put your ticket into the slot(卡槽) of the exit gate and the gate will automatically open,then you can come out.

很简单,您把票投进闸机的卡槽,闸机会自动打开,就可以出去了。

P:Thank you very much!

非常感谢!

M:My pleasure!

不客气!

Dialogue 6

P:Excuse me. Where is the toilet?

打扰一下,请问厕所在哪里?

M:Umm go straight and you will find the toilet on your right side.

嗯,直走你就会发现厕所在你的右边。

P:Oh, thanks!

噢,谢谢你!

M:You're welcome!

不客气!

Dialogue 7

听力6-1

(David is from America. He is at Beijing Railway Station and is finding his way to the Palace Museum.)

David:Excuse me, Miss?

Volunteer:Yes? Is there anything I can do for you?

David:I want to go to the Palace Museum. Can you tell me how to get there?

Volunteer:Sure. You can take subway line 2, get on the train at Beijing Railway Station and get off at Jianguomen Station which is a transfer station, change to line 1 and get off at Tiananmen West Station. You cannot miss it.

David: I beg your pardon? Which station shall I get off to change another line?

Volunteer: Jianguomen Station.

David: Ok, thank you very much.

Volunteer: You're welcome. Have a nice journey.

David: Thanks, bye.

New Words and Expression

automatically[ˌɔtəˈmætɪkli]   adv. 自动地
miss[mis]   v. 错过
station[steiʃn]   n. 车站
transfer station   换乘站
excuse me   打扰一下
Beijing Railway Station   北京火车站
The Palace Museum   故宫博物院

参考地名：

浙一医院 The First Affiliated Hospital, Zhejiang University

浙二医院 The Second Affiliated Hospital, Zhejiang University

浙江省中医院 Zhejiang Provincal Hospital of TCM(Traditional Chinese Medicine 中医)

杭州市中医院 Chinese Medicine Hostipal in Hangzhou

杭州市第一人民医院 Hangzhou First People's Hospital

4.2 买　票

4.2.1 买票充值情景对话

Dialogue 1

M：Hello, can I help you?

你好，有什么可以帮助你吗？

P：It's my first time to take the subway. Can you tell me how to buy a ticket?

这是我第一次乘坐地铁，你能告诉我怎样买票吗？

M：Sure, I can tell you some ways to buy a ticket.

当然可以，我可以告诉你有几种方式乘坐地铁。

P：Wow, that's good.

哇，真好。

M：The first way is to operate on TVM(ticket vending machine) to get a one-way ticket following the instructions. Second, you can buy a ticket at the ticket office where the conductor sells tickets. Thirdly, you can use metro rechargeable card. Just swipe it at the gate, no need to buy tickets anymore. Fourth, you can use an e-metro QR (quick response) code at Alipay, and then scan it directly at the entrance and exit gates. There are still many other ways to operate.

第一种方法是在TVM(自动售票机)上根据提示操作购买。第二,你也可以在售票处买票,有售票员在卖票。第三,使用充值卡,用这种方法,您可以刷卡乘坐地铁,不需要买票了。第四,您可以使用支付宝上的电子地铁乘车码,然后直接在入口和出口上扫描。当然也有很多别的方式可以操作。

P:So I can try any way to take subway.

所以我可以随便选择任何一种方式进站乘地铁。

M:Of course.

是的。

P:Thanks a lot.

非常感谢。

Dialogue 2

P:Excuse me,would you please tell me how to buy a ticket on TVM?

打扰一下,你能告诉我怎样在自动售票机上买票吗?

M:I'm glad to help you. First, select your destination on the route map and the number of tickets, wait until the price information showing on the screen. Then insert coins or banknotes into the slot, 5 and 10 yuan notes only. Last but not least, don't forget to take your tickets and change from the slot.

很高兴帮助您!首先,在路线地图上选好目的地,等到屏幕上出现价格信息,然后投硬币或钱,自动售票机只接受五元、十元的纸币。最后但也很重要,不要忘记从出币口取走你的票和钱。

P:That's too complex, can I buy tickets here?

真复杂,我可以在这买票吗?

M:Sorry, this is Customer Service Center. We only deal with enquiries. But the volunteer wearing a red vest can help you in detail.

不行,这里是客服中心,我们只负责解答疑惑,不过那边穿红马甲的志愿者可以给您提供详细帮助。

P:I am grateful for the information you have provided.

感谢你提供的信息。

M:It's my duty.

别客气,这是我的责任。

Dialogue 3

P:Why can't I buy a ticket on the ticket vending machine?

为什么我不能在自动售票机上买票?

M: I'm sorry, the TVM can't work now, you can buy tickets at the ticket office.

很抱歉，自动售票机出了故障。你可以在人工售票亭买票。

P: Alright.

好的。

M: Where would you like to go?

你要去哪里？

P: West Lake Culture Square.

西湖文化广场。

M: How many tickets do you want?

你要买几张票？

P: Two tickets.

两张票。

M: Six yuan in all.

一共六元。

P: Here you are.

给你。

M: This is your tickets and change.

这是您的票和零钱。

P: Thank you!

谢谢你！

M: You are welcome!

不客气！

Dialogue 4

P: Excuse me, where can I get the ticket?

不好意思，我在哪里买票呢？

M: You can get it at the Ticket Center. Please line up at the Ticket Center.

您可以在票务中心买票，请在这里排队。

P: What kind of ticket should I buy?

我应该买哪种车票呢？

M: You can choose the stored-value ticket or single journey ticket. Usually, the SVT is sold at the Ticket Center, and the single journey ticket is sold on the Ticket Vending Machine.

您可以选择储值票或者单程票，通常，储值票在票务中心买，单程票在自动售票机上买。

P: How long is the validity period of a single journey ticket?

单程票的有效期是多久？

M: The single journey ticket is valid at the right day.

单程票在当天的运营时间内有效。

Dialogue 5

P: Where can I recharge my card, please?

请问交通卡充值在哪里?

M:You can recharge it through the automatic value-added machine or the Customer Service Center.

请通过自动充值机客服中心充值。

P:Please tell me how to recharge my card on AVM(automatic value-added machine,自动充值机).

请告诉我如何给在AVM上给储值卡充值?

M:I'm glad to help you. First, click the add value button on AVM. Second, insert your stored value card in the slot, then choose payment method, Alipay or cash are supported, click the confirmation button after you seeing the value information on the screen. Finally, take out your stored value card.

很高兴帮助您!首先,请按自动充值机上的充值键,然后插入储值卡,然后选择支付方式,支付宝或现金都支持,查看完屏幕显示的金额信息后,按确认键,充值成功,取回您的储值卡。

P:Oh, I got it. Thanks a lot!

我明白了,非常感谢!

M:You are welcome!

不客气!

Dialogue 6

P:Excuse me, is there any ticket or card like Octopus card in Hong Kong?

请问这里有像香港八达通之类的储值卡吗?

M:Yes, we have Hangzhou Tong card. You can buy it in the Customer Service Center.

我们这里有杭州通。您可以在客服中心购买。

Dialogue 7

P:I want to recharge my store value card.

我想给储值卡充值。

M:How much would you like to recharge?

请问您想充多少钱?

P:I want to put 50 yuan in my card.

我想往我的卡里充50元。

M:OK, please hang on. It's done. There is 50 yuan in your card now, please have a check.

好的,请稍等。可以了。现在您的卡上有50元钱,请确认一下。

P:Thank you!

谢谢!

M:You are welcome!

不客气!

Dialogue 8

M:Hello, what can I do for you?

你好,有什么可以帮助你吗?

P:I want to recharge 100 RMB to my card.

我想充值 100 元。

M:Take cash 100 yuan and recharge 100 yuan to your card, the balance now is 115 yuan. Here you are.

收取你现金 100 元,充值 100 元,您卡内余额 115 元。请收好你的卡。

P:Can you give the invoice?

能给我发票吗?

M:Sorry, I can only provide receipt now. You can ask for invoice in the Customer Service Center.

现在我只能提供小票。您去客服中心可索取发票。

P:Oh, I got it. Thanks a lot!

我明白了,非常感谢!

M:You are welcome!

不客气!

Dialogue 9

听力 6-2

(A passenger doesn't know how to use automatic fare collection in subway station, he asks the station operator for help.)

Passenger:Excuse me, would you please tell me how I can buy a ticket?

Station operator:I'm glad to offer help. First of all, let me show you some basic equipment for ticket selling. This way, please.

Passenger:Ok, thanks.

Station operator:This is AVM, or you can call it TVM. Select station of departure and destination, press OK button, then put the cash in, don't forget to take your ticket and change.

Passenger:Oh, I see. How can I use the ticket?

Station operator:Here, this is AGM(automatic gate machine,自动闸门机). Put the ticket in magnetic area, then you'll hear a beep sound, go through as soon as the door opens.

Passenger:Sounds a little bit complex.

Station operator:Don't worry, if you need help, call for us at any time. Oh, one more thing, be sure to put away the ticket and we'll collect it when you arrive at your destination.

Passenger:Thanks a lot.

Station operator:It's my pleasure. Have a nice journey.

New Words and Expressions

equipment [ikwipmənt]	n. 设备
departure [dipɑːtʃə]	n. 出发站
destination [destineiʃn]	n. 目的地
press [pres]	v. 按下
change [tʃeindʒ]	n. 零钱
magnetic [mægnetik]	adj. 有磁性的
complex ['kɔmpleks]	adj. 复杂
Have a nice journey!	旅途愉快!
station operator	站务员

4.2.2 换卡退卡情景对话

Dialogue 1

P: Excuse me, my card doesn't work. Where can I replace it?
您好,我的一卡通坏了,该去哪换呢?
M: We can't do it here. You may go to Chengzhan Station to replace it.
这儿换不了,你得到城站站去换。
P: Can I have the refund for card cost?
能退卡的工本费吗?
M: If the card is damaged, its cost cannot be refunded.
如果卡有损伤,卡的工本费就不能退了。
P: How about the balance on my card?
那卡里的余额呢?
M: The balance will be transferred to your new card.
卡里的余额会转到新卡里。

Dialogue 2

P: Excuse me, I lost my card. What can I do?
您好,我的卡丢了该怎么办?
M: I'm sorry. The card is non-registered. You have to apply for a new one.
抱歉,卡片是不记名的。您得再办一张。
P: OK. I want to do that now. Besides, if my card breaks, can I replace it?
好吧。我现在就要办一张。还有,如果卡坏了可以换吗?
M: Yes, you can bring your card and receipt to replace it at Chengzhan Station.
您可以带上您的卡和收据到城站地铁站换。

4.3　提供信息和帮助

4.3.1　机器故障情景对话

Dialogue 1

M：Good morning. Can I help you?

早上好。我能帮您吗?

P：Good morning. What's wrong with this machine?

早上好。这台机器怎么了?

M：This TVM is out of service. Please go to another one to buy a single ticket.

这台自动售票机暂停服务,请到另一台售票机上去购单程票。

P：I can't buy one all the same. Why doesn't it take my money?

还是买不了,这台机器怎么不收我的钱?

M：Sorry. The note is too worn for the machine to recognize.

不好意思,这钱太旧了导致机器无法识别。

P：But I don't have any more money. What shall I do?

我身上没有别的钱了。我该怎么办?

M：You can buy tickets at the ticket booth over there.

您可以去那边的票亭试试。

P：Oh，I see. Thank you!

我明白了,谢谢!

M：It doesn't matter!

没关系!

Dialogue 2

P：Excuse me，I put the ticket into the slot but it was rejected.

打扰一下,我的票投进去又被退出来了是怎么回事?

M：Would you please let me check your ticket? … You come from Sanba Station and the fee should be 4 yuan but the balance of your token is 2 yuan. Please give 2 yuan more here.

让我验下您的票,好吗?……您从三坝来这儿票价4元,但您的余额是2元,需补2元。

P：I see. Here you are.

明白了,给你。

Dialogue 3

P：Please tell me why the ticket doesn't come out of the TVM?

我想知道为什么票没有从自动售票机中出来?

M：Don't worry. Let me check it. Maybe there is something wrong with the machine.

I will call the repairman. Please wait a moment. I'm sorry, delay your time.

别担心,让我来帮你看看。可能是机器出故障了。我请维修人员来检查一下,请稍等。很抱歉,耽误了您的时间。

Dialogue 4

P:What happened? I can't get through the gate.

怎么回事?我出不了闸机。

M:You are going in the wrong way. Using your right hand to hold the ticket when exit.

您走的是错误路线。您应该用右手持票通过检票机。

Dialogue 5

P:Excuse me! Why did I insert coins but no ticket came out of this TVM?

打扰一下!为什么我在自动售票机里投了币,却没有出票?

M:Don't worry. We need to check it and confirm the situation. If just like you said, we will offer you a free single-journey ticket.

别着急,我们需要检查确认一下,如果真是这样,我们会给您提供一张免费的单程票。

Dialogue 6

P:What's the matter? Why hasn't the train arrived yet?

出什么事了?为什么列车还没有到?

M:Sorry to keep you waiting. There must be something wrong. Please wait patiently. If you are in a hurry, you can change another transportation.

抱歉让您久等,列车可能出现故障。请耐心等候!如果您有急事,可以转乘其他交通工具。

P:How about my ticket?

我的票怎么办?

M:We can return the fare.

我们可以办理退票手续。

Dialogue 7

P:Please tell me why the subway doesn't come? I am afraid that I can't catch the train!

请告诉我为什么地铁还没有来?我恐怕快赶不上火车了!

M:There must be something wrong when the subway is running.

可能列车在运行途中出了点问题。

P:What should I do?

那我要怎么办呢?

M:First, you can return the ticket, and then take a taxi to the train station to change the train ticket. We apologize for any inconvenience.

你可以先退票,再坐出租车去火车站改签火车票。对于列车故障给您带来的不便我们感到非常抱歉。

Dialogue 8

M:Shalom(希伯来语的问候),what can I do for you?

您好,请问有什么需要帮助的吗?

P:I want to return my ticket.

我想要退票。

M:OK. Please wait a moment. This is your refund. Please keep it.

好的,请稍等。这是您的退票费。请您收好。

P:Thanks.

谢谢。

Dialogue 9

P:Excuse me, I put my single ticket into the slot just now but the door did not open.

打扰一下,我刚刚把单程票投进回收口但门没开。

M:I am sorry. Can you point out the gate?

抱歉,您能指出是哪个闸机吗?

P:(Pointing out) This one over there.

(指出)那边那个闸机。

M:Oh, I got it. I will inform the AFC (automatic fare collection,自动售检票系统) maintenance man to check this turnstile. Please sign your name in this form and I'll give you a free ticket to get out.

我知道了。我会通知AFC维修人员来检查这台旋转栅门。请在单上签名,我给您发张免费出站票。

Dialogue 10

听力 6-3

(A visitor is now at the Information Center, he is asking for the way to Wangfujing.)

Conductor:What can I do for you, sir?

Visitor:Could you tell me how to get to Wangfujing? I just can't figure it out from the subway system at all.

Conductor:You take the downtown line 5 train and get off at Dongdan. Dongdan station is a transfer station. Then you take the line 1 train and get off at Wangfujing.

Visitor:Thank you. How much is the fare?

Conductor:A flat fare of RMB(¥)2.00 with unlimited transfers applies to all lines except the Airport Express, which costs ¥25. Children below 1.2 meters in height ride for free when accompanied by a paying adult.

Visitor:Ok, please give me one ticket for me and my baby. How do I use this ticket?

Conductor:You swipe it to get through the AFC machine. And insert it when you leave the subway.

Visitor:By the way, how can I find the way to get out of the platform after I get off the train?

Conductor: That's very easy. The exits are always open, and there are signs.
Visitor: Thank you very much.
Conductor: I'm very happy to help.

New Words and Expressions

downtown [ˌdaun'taun]	adj. 市中心(的)
fare [fɛə]	n. (交通工具的)票价
unlimited [ʌn'limitid]	adj. 无限制的,无约束的
transfer [træns'fəː]	v. 换车,转车
apply [ə'plai]	v. 应用,实施
accompany [ə'kʌmpəni]	v. 陪同,伴随
adult [ə'dʌlt]	n. 成年人
swipe [swaip]	v. 在解码器上刮刷(卡)
insert [in'səːt]	v. 插入,嵌入
platform ['plæt,fɔːm]	n. 月台
figure out	理解,搞清楚
flat fare	单一票制

4.3.2 其他帮助

Dialogue 1

听力 6-4

(Xiao Ming is taking subway for the first time. Xiao Li shows him some equipments in subway station.)

Xiao Ming: Excuse me, I am taking subway for the first time. There are so much modern equipment in subway station that I'm puzzled. Would you be so kind to tell me what it is?

Xiao Li: Sure. Subway transportation has developed rapidly during the past few years. We are in Gongyixiqiao Station on line 4.

Xiao Ming: Oh, I see. What's that? Many people are queuing there.

Xiao Li: That is automatic vending machine. People can buy tickets by themselves.

Xiao Ming: How does that work?

Xiao Li: Let me show you. Put your ticket here and then the door will open after "beep" sound, go through the door you'll get in the subway station.

Xiao Ming: How convenient it is! Now we're arriving at concourse. Look, how bright it is!

Xiao Li: Be cautious not to cross the yellow line when you're waiting for the train.

Xiao Ming: Thank you very much.

Xiao Li: It's my pleasure.

New Words and Expressions

modern [mɔdən]	adj. 现代化的
equipment [ikwipmənt]	n. 设备
transportation [ˌtrænspɔːteiʃn]	n. 交通运输
queue [kjuː]	v. 排队
convenient [kənviːnjnt]	adj. 便利的
concourse [ˈkɔŋkɔːs]	n. 站厅
cautious [kɔːʃəs]	adj. 谨慎的
automatic vending machine	自动售票机

Dialogue 2

听力 6-5

(Xiaohong is a student, she wants to be a volunteer of the subway. She is talking about this with her friend Xiaoming.)

Xiaohong: My English is poor. I don't think I can help with the English service.

Xiaoming: You can do something else.

Xiaohong: I just don't know what else I can do, any suggestions?

Xiaoming: You can give directions to the riders, change coins, help them to buy tickets or recharge their smart cards.

Xiaohong: Anything challenging?

Xiaoming: Help the riders in using the machines, including the automatic fare collection system, automatic analyzer, wheelchair lift and so on. Tell the valid ticket riders how to deal with it.

Xiahong: It's really a great deal I can do.

Xiaoming: Sometimes they have some special services, for example they prepare some slippers for the riders who drop their shoes.

Xiaohong: Can I help to bring the shoes back?

Xiaoming: It's too dangerous, you should follow the instructions: inform the staff immediately.

New Words and Expressions

Volunteer [ˌvɔlənˈtiə]	n. 志愿者
Suggestion [səˈdʒestʃən]	n. 建议
Direction [diˈrekʃən]	n. 方向
Recharge [riːˈtʃɑːdʒ]	v. 再次充值
Challenge [ˈtʃælindʒ]	n. 挑战
Slippers [ˈslipə]	n. 拖鞋
Immediately [iˈmiːdiətli]	adv. 立即
wheelchair lift	残疾人牵引车

Dialogue 3

听力 6-6

(Li Ping is a freshman at metro company, she is on broadcasting duty. She is discussing with her colleague Han Dong.)

Li Ping: Hello, Han Dong. Would you please do me a favor?

Han Dong: Sure, what's the matter?

Li Ping: I am new here and my duty is to broadcast, but I am puzzled by some broadcasting terms. I wonder if you could help me.

Han Dong: Go ahead.

Li Ping: If there is something wrong with station equipment, what shall I do to let passengers know about it?

Han Dong: In that case, you could broadcast as "Your attention please. Please follow staff directions to enter as the (equipment) is not working. We apologize for any inconvenience this might cause."

Li Ping: How can I deal with emergency broadcasting?

Han Dong: "Your attention please! This is an emergency. Please leave the station immediately." or "Your attention please. This is an emergency. Please follow directions and leave the station immediately. Remain calm. Don't run."

Li Ping: Thank you. One more question, how should I deal with terminated service?

Han Dong: "Your attention please. Train service is suspended because (incident). We apologize for any inconvenience this might cause."

Li Ping: I really appreciate your English pronunciation. Thanks a lot.

Han Dong: That's all right.

New Words and Expressions

broadcast [ˈbrɔːdkɑːst]	n.	广播
passenger [ˈpæsindʒə]	n.	乘客
attention [əˈtenʃən]	n.	注意
staff [stɑːf]	n.	工作人员
apologize [əˈpɒlədʒaiz]	v.	道歉
inconvenience [ˌinkənˈviːnjəns]	n.	不便
cause [kɔːz]	v.	引起
emergency [iˈməːdʒənsi]	n.	紧急情况
terminate [ˈtəːmineit]	v.	终止
do somebody a favor		帮忙

Dialogue 4

M: Hello, may I help you?
您好,请问有什么需要帮忙的吗?

P: Yes, I'd like to report a lost backpack. I left it on the train.

是的,我想报失一个背包。我把它落在列车上了。

M: I am so sorry to hear that. Please tell me the arrival time and direction of the train.

我很遗憾。请问那趟列车的方向和时间。

P: Well, the train just left the station a minute ago.

好,就是一分钟之前离开的那趟列车。

M: I see. Can you describe your backpack?

我明白了,您能描述一下您的背包吗?

P: It's a black and leathery one which contains my wallet and some files.

它是一个黑色的皮革背包,里面装了我的钱包和一些文件。

M: Well, we will try our best to find it. Would you tell me your name and phone number? I'll contact you as soon as we find it.

我们会尽全力去找到它。能告诉我您的名字和电话号码吗?我们一找到就会与您联系。

Dialogue 5

P: Excuse me, my friend has a bad headache.

对不起,我的朋友头疼得很厉害。

M: Please lie on the bench and have a rest. Let me call the Emergency Center.

请躺在长椅上休息一下。我来拨打急救中心的电话。

P: Is it open now?

急救中心现在还开着吗?

M: Yes, it opens round-the-clock.

开着的,它全天 24 小时服务。

P: Thanks a lot!

非常感谢!

M: My pleasure!

这是我的荣幸

Dialogue 6

M: Your luggage is too heavy. Let me give you a hand.

您的行李太重了,让我来帮您拿吧?

P: It's very kind of you.

你太好了。

M: You are welcome. If you have any trouble, please feel free to contact the station staffs. It is our pleasure to serve you.

不客气,如果您还有什么困难请与车站工作人员联系,我们都很乐意为您服务。

Dialogue 7

P: Oh, my god! My umbrella fell into the track.

天哪！我的雨伞掉进轨道里去了。

M：Take it easy, we will help you.

别紧张，我们将帮助您

P：Can I take it back at once?

我能马上拿回它吗？

M：Sorry, I'm afraid that we can't pick up your umbrella immediately because it's the running line.

对不起，我想我们不能马上拾回您的雨伞，因为这是运营线路。

P：But when can I take it back?

那我什么时候可以拿回它？

M：We just can get it in no-traffic hours. Don't worry, we will return it to you as soon as we pick it up.

我们只能在非运营时间拿回，别担心，我们一拾回它就会完整无缺地归还给您。

Dialogue 8

M：Excuse me, you can't go down the platform and take the train now.

对不起，您现在不能下站台搭地铁。

P：Why? What happened?

为什么？发生什么事了？

M：The train is out of service. All passengers are requested to leave the station now.

列车暂停服务，所有的乘客请现在离开车站。

P：But I have bought the fare.

但是我已经买了票。

M：You can return the token to the Customer Service Center.

您可以去客服中心退票。

Dialogue 9

P：What is the matter? I swipe the card but I can't enter in.

怎么回事？我刷了卡，但是我进不去。

M：Let me check it for you. The ticket is invalid, please ask the Customer Service Center for help. Follow me, please.

让我帮你看看吧。这张票已失效，请咨询客服中心，请您跟我来。

P：You have to pay one yuan more for insufficient ticket price.

票价不足，您应该补1元。

M：Here you are.

给你。

P：This is your new card. Please keep it well.

这是你的新票。请保管好。

Dialogue 10

P：Hello! Could you tell me what can I do for you?

您好！请问有什么可以帮您的？

M:Hello! What's wrong with this gate?

你好！这个闸机怎么了？

P:Let me check it for you. Your ticket is invalid. Please follow me to the Customer Service Center.

让我帮你看看。这个票已经失效了,请跟我到客服中心办理。

P:OK. Thank you!

好的。谢谢！

M:It's my pleasure!

这是我的荣幸！

Dialogue 11

P:What's wrong with my ticket?

我的车票怎么了？

M:Your ticket is overtaken, please pay the exact fare.

您的车票超乘了,请付足车费。

Dialogue 12

P:What can I do if I put the coins into TVM, but no ticket comes out?

我投币到自动售票机但没出票怎么办？

M:Don't worry, if it happened, the station attendant would give you a free single ticket, after we confirm this situation.

别着急,如果是这样,经过站务员确认后,会免费给您一张单程票。

Dialogue 13

P:Hello, when is the first train to Pedestrian Street?

您好,请问到步行街的首班车是几点？

M:Now your position is in library, the first train is 6:33.

现在您所在的位置是图书馆,首班车时间为6:33。

P:And when is the last train?

那请问末班车的时间呢？

M:The last train is 22:42.

末班车的时间为22:42。

P:Thanks!

谢谢！

M:You are welcome. I wish you a happy voyage.

不用,祝您一路顺风。

Dialogue 14

P:How often does the subway run?

请问地铁多久一趟啊？

M:The subways are running on a five-minute headway.

每隔5分钟一趟。

P:Why doesn't the train come?

那为什么还不来啊?

M:Sir, it's already 23:00, the last subway to Train Station is 22:42.

先生,现在已经23点了,去往火车站方向末班车的时间为22:42。

P:So is it. Thank you.

原来是这样,谢谢。

Dialogue 15

P:How long is about the train headway now?

列车间隔是几分钟?

M:In rush hours, the train headway is 3 minutes; at off-peak time, it's 5 minutes.

在高峰期,列车的间隔是3分钟;在非高峰期,列车的间隔是5分钟。

Dialogue 16

P:Excuse me, when will the next train arrive?

请问下一班车什么时候到?

M:About 3 minutes, please wait a moment.

大概3分钟,请稍等。

P:How often does the train run?

请问列车间隔是多少?

M:Around every 10 minutes.

大约10分钟。

4.4 安全工作

4.4.1 安全标志和指示

安全标志和指示如 Table 4-1、Table 4-2、Table 4-3 所示。

Table 4-1 安全标志和指示 1

Mind Your Hand 当心夹手	Mind the Gap 当心缝隙	Hold the Handrail 紧握扶手	Do Not Retrograde 禁止逆行	Please Keep Clear 请勿停留

续表

Table 4-2 安全标志和指示 2

Emergency Unlock
紧急装置
Emergency Use Only
仅在紧急情况下使用
STEP 1: Open the cover
第 1 步：打开罩板
STEP 2: Switch to 1(brake)
第 2 步：按箭头旋至①制动
STEP 3: When the train stop, switch to 2 to unlock the door
第 3 步：列车停稳后，再旋至②解锁车门
Anyone who operates without authorization will be held responsible in accordance with the law!
擅自动用，依法追究责任！

续表

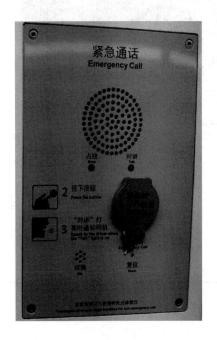	Emergency Call 紧急通话 Busy　　Talk 占线　　对讲 1. Lift the cover during emergency 紧急时打开此盖 2. Press the button 按下按钮 3. Speak to the driver when the "Talk" light is on "对讲"灯亮时通知司机 Mic　　Reset 话筒　　复位 Passengers shall bear liabilities for non-emergency use 非紧急情况下使用将负法律责任
	Emergency Door Release 紧急开门 1. Remove the transparent plate 移除透明罩板 2. Turn handle to "Request" position 旋转手柄至"请求"位 3. Wait until train comes to a complete stop, turn handle to "Unlock" position 待列车停稳后,旋转手柄至"解锁"位 4. Pull door open 手动来开车门 Passengers shall bear legal liabilities for non-emergency use 非紧急情况下使用将负法律责任

Table 4-3 安全标志和指示 3

Dangerous Articles Forbidden

严禁携带易燃易爆等危险品进站

Caution Wet Floor	Emergency Stop Button	Explosion-Proof Tank	
小心地滑	紧急停止按钮	防爆罐	

Above row (upper): | | | Emergency Exit | Fire Extinguisher |
| | | 紧急出口 | 灭火器 |

4.4.2 情景对话

Dialogue 1

听力 6-7

(Hubert is from London. He is talking about the safety on the London underground with Xiaoli.)

Xiaoli: Is there a security check in London?

Hubert: Yes, we do this check after the explosion on July 7th, 2005.

Xiaoli: I think this is inconvenient, I don't know whether it is worthing the time or not.

Hubert: . Safety first, precaution crucial.

Xiaoli: is there any other ways to prevent accidents in London?

Hubert: Of course, there are several safety warnings given to passengers, such as the "mind the gap" announcement and the regular announcements for passengers to "keep behind the yellow line".

Xiaoli: How about the crowd?

Hubert: Relatively few accidents are caused by overcrowding on the platforms and staff monitors platforms and passageways at busy times to prevent people entering the system if they become overcrowded.

Xiaoli: I see, we never do too much for our safety.

New Words and Expressions

explosion [ikˈspləuʒn]	n. 爆炸
inconvenient [ˌinkənˈviːnjənt]	adj. 不方便的
prevent [priˈvent]	v. 预防
warning [ˈwɔːniŋ]	n. 警告
announcement [əˈnaunsmənt]	n. 通告
regular [ˈregjulə]	adj. 经常的
crowd [kraud]	n. 人群
relatively [ˈrelətivli]	adv. 相关的
cause [kɔːz]	n. 原因
overcrowding [ˌəuvəˈkraud]	v. 过度拥挤
staff [staːf]	n. （全体）工作人员
monitor [ˈmɔnitə]	v. 监测、监控
platform [ˈplætˌfɔːm]	n. 站台
mind the gap	小心台阶间跨度
precaution crucial	预防为主
security check	安全检查

Dialogue 2

听力 6-8

(David and Sam are discussing about ATP in metro system.)

David：What is the full name for ATP?

Sam：It is Automatic Train Protection.

David：What is the function of it?

Sam：It is a device used to ensure train's safe operation.

David：But what is the relationship between ATP and ATC，ATO，ATS?

Sam：It is the foundation of entire ATC system. ATO and ATS subsystem relies on ATP system.

David：Can you introduce its working principle?

Sam：ATP system can automatically detect train's running location，then it ensures the greatest running speed，achieving speeding protection. In this way，it can ensure the regular intervals(间隔).

列车自动保护系统可以自动检测火车的运行位置,然后确保最大的运行速度,实现超速保护。这样可以确保常规间隔。

New Words and Expressions

function [fʌnkʃən]	n. 职务,功能,作用
foundation [faundeiʃən]	n. 基础,基座
subsystem [sʌbsistəm]	n. 子系统
principle [prinsəpl]	n. 原则,原理
detect [ditekt]	vt. 察觉,发现,探测
speeding [spi:diŋ]	n. 超速行车
ATP(Automatic Train Protection)	n. 列车自动保护装置
ATO(Automatic Train Operation)	列车自动操作系统
ATS(Automatic Train Supervision)	列车自动监控系统
ATC(Automatic Train Control System)	列车自动控制系统

ATC=ATO+ATP+ATS

Dialogue 3

听力 6-9

(David and Sam are discussing metro safety.)

David: What factors may cause metro operation malfunction?

Sam: Capacity, vehicle, signal, track, power supply, etc.

David: What do you mean by capacity?

Sam: In big city, great capacity during rush hour may cause passengers hurt.

David: Oh, then how can it be improved in case of that?

Sam: Platform Screen Doors are installed on the platform, which is synchronized with train doors' opening and closing.

David: We need not only improve our technology, but improve our safety consciousness.

Sam: Right. There are a lot of guide signs and special working staff on every platform to evacuate passengers.

David: So it is very important to be safe every time and everywhere.

Sam: Absolutely.

New Words and Expressions

malfunction [mælfʌnkʃən]	n. 故障
Consciousness [kɔnʃəsnis]	n. 意识
improve [impru:v]	vt. 改进,改善
evacuate [ivækjueit]	vt. 疏散
Synchronize [siŋkrənaiz]	v. 与……同步

rush hour 高峰时间
platform screen doors 屏蔽门

Dialogue 4

听力 6-10

FAS 火灾报警系统

(David is from America. He is talking about Beijing Subway with Mr. Zhang.)

David: Can you tell me the full name of FAS?

Mr. Zhang: Sure. FAS mean Fire Alarm System.

David: So what is the function of it?

Mr. Zhang: Well, it has at least three functions, such as fire alarm, automatic spray and extinguishing, alarm linkage.

好的,这个至少具有三项功能,例如火灾报警,自动喷雾和灭火,报警联动。

David: Then what does FAS consist of?

Mr. Zhang: Basically it contains a supervising and managing center, control panel, floor display, detector, control module and manual alarm.

基本上,它包含一个监督和管理中心、控制面板、地板显示器、检测器、控制模块和手动报警器。

David: And can you tell me its working principle?

你能告诉我它的工作原理吗

Mr. Zhang: Once the detector measures smoke, it will automatically send alarm signal. And it will activate automatic spray device to extinguish fire in time.

一旦探测器检测到烟雾,它将自动发送警报信号,并启动自动喷雾装置,及时扑灭火灾。

David: Oh, it seemed that FAS has a perfect function.

哦,看来火灾报警系统具有完善的功能。

Mr. Zhang: Right. As this is because subway is an underground transport, it will cause great loss once fire cannot be extinguished in time.

对。这是因为地铁是地下交通工具,一旦无法及时熄灭,将会造成巨大的损失。

New Words and Expressions

spray [sprei] vt. 喷淋
linkage [liŋkidʒ] n. 连接,连锁,联动
display [displei] vt. 陈列,显示,展出
detector [ditektə] n. 探测器
manual [mænjuəl] adj. 体力的,手控的
smoke [sməuk] n. 烟雾
loss [lɔs] n. 损失,亏损

extinguish [ikstiŋgwiʃ]	vt.	熄灭,扑灭
underground [ʌndəgraund]	adj.	地下的
FAS：Fire Alarm System		火灾报警系统
extinguish fire		灭火

Dialogue 5

听力 6-11

(David and John are talking about metro signaling.)

David：Do you know the components of the metro signaling system?

您知道地铁信号系统的组成部分吗?

John：It contains seven parts, moving block system, train testing system, station signal interlock system, train operation control system, ATP system, ATO system and ATS system.

它包括七个部分,移动闭塞系统、列车测试系统、车站信号互锁系统、列车运行控制系统、列车自动保护装置系统、列车自动操作系统和列车自动监控系统系统。

David：Can subway run safely with signal system?

地铁可以通过信号系统安全运行吗?

John：Yes, it is not only safe for metro operation, but also convenient for passengers.

是的,它不仅对地铁运营安全,而且对乘客也很方便。

David：Do you mean the train information display on the platform?

您的意思是平台上显示的火车信息?

John：Right. You can read when the next train will arrive, and the route line direction, etc.

对。您可以阅读下一班火车的到达时间、路线方向等信息。

David：And sometimes mobile TV is shown on the screen.

有时屏幕上会显示移动电视。

John：On the one hand, there is some basic information about subway. On the other hand, it scrolls some broadcast about weather report, road condition, and etc.

一方面,有一些关于地铁的基本信息。另一方面,它滚动播放一些有关天气预报、道路状况等的广播。

David：How convenient the system is!

系统太方便了吧!

New Words and Expressions

block [blɔk]	n.	闭塞
interlock [intəlɔk]	n.	连锁
convenient [kənviːnjənt]	adj.	方便的

display [displei]	n. 显示器
passenger [pæsindʒə]	n. 乘客
scroll [skrəul]	vt. 滚动
broadcast [brɔːdkɑːst]	vt. 广播,播放
mobile TV	移动电视
metro signaling	地铁信号系统

Dialogue 6

听力 6-12

Telecommunication System 通信系统

(David and John are talking about communication system in metro system.)

David: What are the main components for metro telecommunication system?

地铁通信系统的主要组件是什么?

John: Transmission system, wireless system, public official telephone system, Inner station and line-side telephone system and dispatch system.

传输系统、无线系统、公用电话系统、内站和线路侧电话系统和调度系统。

David: What is wireless system used for?

无线系统是做什么用的?

John: As every car is a moving object, communication lines are impossible. Wireless communication is adopted.

由于每辆车都是移动物体,所以有线的通信线路是不可能的。适合采用无线通信。

David: Well, how does the communication process achieve?

那么,沟通过程如何实现?

John: Every station has a machine room with a switch connecting control center, in charge of train control signals' receiving and sending.

每个站都有一个机房,机房带有一个连接控制中心的开关,负责列车控制信号的接收和发送。

David: What kind of communication medium is used?

使用哪种通信介质?

John: It is advanced fiber. It has great shield performance, fast transmission speed and good privacy.

它是高级光纤。具有良好的屏蔽性能,传输速度快、保密性好。

David: It seems that it is a wonderful system.

看来这是一个很棒的系统。

New Words and Expressions

telecommunication [telikəmjuːniˈkeiʃən]   n. 电信,通信

transmission [trænsˈmiʃən]	n. 传送,传输
wireless [ˈwaiəlis]	adj. 无线的
official [əˈfiʃəl]	adj. 公务上的,官方的
switch [switʃ]	n. 交换机,开关
fiber [ˈfaibə]	n. 光纤,纤维
shield [ʃiːld]	n. 屏蔽
privacy [ˈpraivəsi]	n. 私密性,保密性
machine room	机房

4.5 行车组织原则

4.5.1 行车组织原则

地铁采用右侧行车制行车,司机人工驾驶列车运行时以右侧信号为准。

The right-hand driving system is adopted in metro. Operators obey signals on the right hand when he operates a train in manual mode.

(1) 行车时间,从零时起计算,实行 24 小时制。行车日期划分:以零时为界,零时以前办妥的行车手续,零时以后仍视为有效。

The operation time, starting from zero hour. Operation dates shall be divided by zero hour, which means that any operation procedures completed prior to zero hour will become invalid after zero hour.

(2) 正常情况下列车运行采用自动驾驶模式。

The normal operation of train adopts the mode of ATO.

(3) 出、入段线属正线管理范围,列车出厂前需与行调联系凭行调指令和信号显示出厂。

Arriving and leaving tracks are in the range of main track management. Before leaving the depots, the train shall get contact with the operation dispatcher and leave in accordance with the instruction of the operation dispatcher and the signal display.

(4) 指挥列车在正线运行的命令只能由行调发布,列车司机、车站值班员接受行调的指挥和命令。

Only the operation dispatcher is permitted to issue transportation instructions requiring trains to run in the main track. Train drivers and attendants on station commands and instructions from the operation dispatcher.

(5) 空车、调试车、工程车和救援列车出、入车厂均按列车办理。

Procedures for unloaded trains, debugging trains, engineering trains and rescue trains accessing depot shall be handled as trains.

(6) 人工报点时,列车到、发、通过时刻的确认时机规定如下:到达时刻,以列车在站台规定位置停稳时为准;出发时刻,以列车在站台启动不再停车时为准;通过时刻,以列车头部离开站台时为准。

If the arrival time, departure time and through time of trains are reported by people, they shall be confirmed at the following time: the arrival time shall be the time at which a train parked on the position required by the platform; the departure time shall be the time at which the train starts up on the platform; through time shall be the time at which the train head leaves the platform.

(7) 列车运行采用司机在前端正向牵引运行的方式。

During the operation of train, the driver shall tract running at the front end.

(8) 列车晚点统计方法:比照运营时刻表单程每列延误300秒以下为正常,300秒及以上为晚点。

Method for late arrival statistics: it is normal for a train to delay less than 300 seconds in a single trip in comparsion with the operation schedule. Any delay for 300 seconds or more shall be deemed as late arrival.

4.5.2 行车指挥

1. 行车组织和指挥机构

(1) 行车指挥执行层次。

Structure for implementation of operation commanding

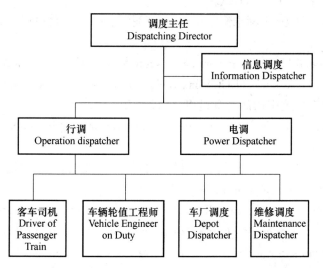

(2) 运行控制中心(OCC)

Operating Control Center (OCC)

运行控制中心是日常管理、设备维修、行车组织的指挥中心,设有调度主任、行调、电调、维修调度员,通过各工种调度员对列车运营及设备运行情况进行监视、指挥、协调和调度。

The operating control center is an command center for routine operation management, equipment maintenance and operation organization. It sets up positions including control director, operation dispatcher, power dispatcher and construction dispatcher. They supervise, command, coordinate and dispatch the trains and equipment operation. Functions of the control center mainly include:

1) 行调负责日常行车运营的人工调度指挥工作,实现按时刻表行车,达到"安全、准时、高效、快捷"的目标。

Operation dispatcher is responsible for manual dispatching and commanding of daily operation to ensure that all trains run as per the operation schedule and achieving the objectives of "safety, timeliness, effectiveness and rapidness".

2) 行调负责处理在运营过程中出现突发事件及灾害情况时的指挥和恢复。

Operation dispatcher is responsible for handling emergencies occurring in operation, and the commanding and recovering in the cases of disasters.

3) 行调负责运营的组织协调工作,确保人员和财产的安全。

Operation dispatcher is responsible for the organization and coordination of operation, ensuring the safety of people and property.

4) 行调负责运营信息的收发工作。

Operation dispatcher is responsible for the collection and release of operation information.

5) 电调负责供电系统的运行监控。

Power dispatcher is responsible for operation monitoring of the power supply system.

(3) 车厂控制中心(DCC)

Control Center of Depot (DCC)

1) DCC 是车厂管理、车辆维修组织和作业的控制中心,车厂(DCC)设有车辆轮值技术员及车厂调度员。

DCC is the control center for depot management and the organization and operation of vehicle maintenance. A depot (DCC) has vehicle on-duty technicians and depot dispatcher.

2) DCC 负责车厂范围内的行车组织、维修施工管理。

DCC is responsible for the operation organization, maintenance and construction management within the depot.

3) DCC 负责车辆日常检修、清洁、定修和临修工作控制,为轻轨运营及设备维修施工提供数量足够和工况良好的客车和工程列车。

DCC is responsible for controlling the routine maintenance, cleaning and periodical and occasional maintenance of vehicles to provide sufficient quantity of passenger trains and engineering trains in good condition for light rail operation and equipment maintenance and construction.

(4) 车厂信号控制

Signal Control of Depot

车厂设有计算机联锁系统,实现车辆段内安全、完整的联锁关系和进路控制。

A depot sets up a computer interlocking system to ensure safe and integrated interlocking relations and route control within the depot.

2. 行车指挥原则

(1) 行车有关人员必须服从行调指挥,执行行调命令,行调必须严格按《运营时刻表》及《行车组织规则》指挥行车。

All operation-related personnel must obey and implement the instructions of the operation dispatcher, and the operation dispatcher must command the train operation strictly in accordance with the Operation Schedule and Transportation Organization Regulations.

(2) 指挥列车运行的命令,只能由行调发布,发布前应详细了解现场情况,听取有关人员意见。

Only the operation dispatcher can give orders to command the operation of trains. Before giving an order, the operation dispatcher shall know the situation on site in details and hear from relevant personnel.

3. 列车识别号及车次的规定

(1) 客车识别号由服务号、序列号、车组号、目的地号组成。

The identification number of a passenger train consists of service number, serial number, train unit number and destination number.

(2) 序列号:由2位数字组成,表示列车运行顺序及方向顺序,上行为偶数,下行为奇数。

Serial Number: consists of two figures and indicates the operation sequence and direction sequence of a train, even numbers for up trains while odd numbers for down trains.

(3) 车组号:由6位数字组成,代表本列车车底的编号。

Train Unit Number: consists of six figures and indicates the numbers at the bottom of the train.

(4) 目的地号:由4位字母组成,其中第一位代表线路号,第二、三位代表车站号,第四位代表站台编号。

Destination Number: consists of four letters, with the first letter representing the track number, the second and third letters representing the station number, and the fourth letters representing the platform number.

(5) 客车车次:"服务号+序列号",代表通常意义上的客车车次,即客车车次由5位数组成,前3位代表服务号,后2位为代表列车行程。

Passenger Train Number: "Service Number + Serial Number" indicates the passenger train number in the usual sense. That is, the passenger train number consists of five figures, the first three figures represent the service number and the last two figures represent the train route.

(6) 援列车车次由3位数字表示。

Rescue train number consists of three figures.

4.5.3 正线信号控制

Table 4-4 为主轨道的控制信号。

Table 4-4 Signal control of the main track

项目 Item	功能 Function	含义 Meaning	站控状态 Station Control State		中控状态 Center Control State	
			MMI	HMI	MMI	HMI
1	道岔定位 Turnout Fixing	设置道岔处在定位状态,道岔名显示绿色 The turnout is set as position fixed, and the turnout name is displayed in green	×	√	√	×
2	道岔反位 Turnout Reversing	设置道岔处在反位状态,道岔名显示黄色 The turnout is set as on reverse position, and the turnout name is displayed in yellow	×	√	√	×
3	道岔单独锁闭 Separate Locking of Turnout	设置道岔处于单锁状态,使道岔无法被操动,道岔上显示"○" The turnout is set as separately locked, and thus cannot be controlled for operation. It displays "○"	—	√	—	—
4	道岔解锁 Release of Locked Turnout	设置道岔处于解锁状态,无条件地对单独锁闭的道岔进行解锁 The turnout is set as unlocked, which means that turnouts separately locked will be released unconditionally	—	√	—	—
5	重开列车信号 Reopening Train Signals	当进路信号机开放后因故关闭时,若开放条件又满足,执行"重开列车信号"功能,使该信号机重新开放 When a route signal is turned off after startup for certain reasons, if the requirements for startup are satisfied, the signal will open again by implementing the function of "reopening train signals"	×	√	√	×
6	设置进路 Route Setting	通过操作使道岔和区段锁闭,使信号开放的过程 The course of locking turnouts and sections through operations to make signal open	×	√	√	×
7	取消列车进路 Cancel Train Route	当列车还未驶入信号机的接近区段,取消任何列车进路的操作,从而导致进路立即解锁。如以某信号机为始端的进路为自动控,执行"取消列车进路"功能后,将会自动转为人工控 The operation of cancelling any train route handled before a train drives into the approach section of signals, and there by causing the route to be immediately released. If a route with a certain signal as its initial end is automatically controlled, it will automatically turn to manual control after "cancellation of train route"	×	√	√	×

续表

项目 Item	功能 Function	含义 Meaning	站控状态 Station Control State		中控状态 Center Control State	
			MMI	HMI	MMI	HMI
8	人解列车进路 Manual Release of Train Route	当列车驶入信号机的接近区段时,设置的操作总手动解锁或自动解锁,造成进路的解锁延迟250 s。如以某信号机为始端的进路为自动控,执行"人解列车进路"功能后,将会自动转为人工控 The operation of setting general manual release or manual release when a train drives into the approach section of signals, and thereby causing the release of route to be delayed for 250 s. If a route with a certain signal as its initial end is automatically controlled, it will automatically turn to manual control after "manual release of train route"	×	√	√	×
9	信号封锁 Signal Locking	对进路信号机进行封锁,在解除封锁之前,该信号机无法开放但可通过该信号机排列进路 Locking the route signal. The route signal will be unable to open before release of locking. But you can use this signal to set routes	—	√	—	×
10	信号解封 Signal Unlocking	对封锁状态下的信号机进行解除封锁 The locked signal is released	—	√	—	×
11	引导 Guiding	当信号机因故不能正常开放时,可开放引导信号 When a signal is unable to open normally for certain reasons, you can open guiding signals	—	√	—	×
12	设置自动通过进路 Setting Automatic Passthrough Route	设置进路模式为自动通过模式,进路不会因列车驶过而解锁,条件满足后自动开放始端信号 Setting the mode of route as automatic passthrough. The route will not be released for train passing. When the requirements are satisfied, the initial end signals will open automatically	×	√	√	×
13	取消自动通过进路 Cancel Automatic Passthrough Route	取消进路的自动通过模式,但并不会取消进路,进路性质转为基本列车进路 Cancelling the automatic passthrough of route, but not cancelling the route. The nature of route becomes basic train route	×	√	√	×
14	进路交人工控 Manual Control of Route Traffic	取消进路始端信号机的ATS自动触发功能,转为人工控制 Cancelling the ATS automatic trigger function of the route initial end signal and turning to manual handling	×	√	√	×

续表

项目 Item	功能 Function	含义 Meaning	站控状态 Station Control State		中控状态 Center Control State	
			MMI	HMI	MMI	HMI
15	进路交自动控 Automatic Control of Route Traffic	设置进路始端信号机的ATS自动触发功能 Setting the ATS automatic trigger function of the route initial end signal of route	×	√	√	×
16	查询进路控制状态 Enquiry of Control State of Route	查看进路始端信号机是否处于ATS自动触发状态 Checking whether the route initial end signal is in ATS automatic trigger state	√	√	√	√
17	区故解 Section Trouble Shooting	使非正常解锁的轨道区段恢复正常状态 Making track sections that are released improperly to return to normal	—	√	—	×
18	区段跟踪切除 Deactivation of Section Tracing	设置某计轴在切除状态,使ATS不再使用该计轴跟踪列车信息 Setting the axle counter as deactivated, thereby making ATS no longer using this axle counter to trace train information	√	√	√	×
19	区段跟踪激活 Activation of Section Tracing	取消某计轴的切除状态,恢复ATS跟踪列车信息 Cancelling the deactivation of axle counter to reactivate ATS to trace train information	√	√	√	×
20	自动折返 Automatic Turnback	设置列车自动折返进路 Setting the automatic turnback route of trains	×	√	√	×
21	全站封锁 Entire Station Locking	"全站封锁"按钮灯常态不显示,当两台联锁机重启或不同步的状态下切换,"全站封锁"按钮出现并亮红灯。此时全站处于封锁状态,不能对室外的设备进行任何操作 The "entire station locking" button lamp is off at normal times. In the case of reset or nonsynchronous turnout between two interlocking machines, the "entire station locking" button appears and turns red. Now, the entire station is locked, and no operation can be made to outdoor equipment	√	—	—	×
22	上电解锁 Power-on Unlocking	"上电解锁"按钮灯常态不显示。当两台联锁机重启后,"上电解锁"按钮出现并亮红灯,整个联锁区处于锁闭状态 The "power-on unlocking" button lamp is off at normal times. When two interlocking machines reset, the "power-on unlocking" button appears and turns red. Now, the whole interlocking area is locked	√	—	—	×

续 表

项目 Item	功能 Function	含义 Meaning	站控状态 Station Control State		中控状态 Center Control State	
			MMI	HMI	MMI	HMI
23	计轴复位 Resetting of Axle Counter	使联锁机允许 IBP 盘执行计轴预复位操作 Making the interlocking machines to allow IBP disk to implement the pre-resetting of axle counters	—	√	—	×
24	建立进路 Route Creation	等同"排列进路" The same to "route setting"	—	√	—	×
25	总取消 General Cancellation	同"取消列车进路" The same to "cancellation of train route"	—	√	—	×
26	信号重开 Signal Reopening	当信号机开放后因故关闭时,若开放条件又满足,执行"信号重开"命令,使该信号机重新开放 When a signal is turned off after startup for certain reasons, if the requirements for startup are satisfied, the signal will open again by implementing the function of "signal reopening"	×	√	√	×
27	总人解 General Manual Release	同"人解列车进路" The same to "manual release of train route"	—	√	—	×
28	引导按钮 Guiding Button	同"引导" The same to "guiding"	—	√	—	×
29	道岔总定 General Turnout Fixing	同"道岔定位" The same to "turnout fixing"	—	√	—	×
30	道岔总反 General Turnout Reversing	同"道岔反位" The same to "turnout reversing"	—	√	—	×
31	道岔单锁 Separate Locking of Turnout	同"道岔单独锁闭" The same to "separate locking of turnout"	—	√	—	×
32	封锁按钮 "Locking" Button	用于执行"信号封锁"或"信号解封"操作的按钮 The button for "signal locking" and "signal unlocking" operations	—	√	—	×
33	命令清除 Command Clear	取消所要执行的功能 Canceling the function to be implemented	—	√	—	√

第 5 章　其他专业英语

5.1　系统中英文提示及解析

Linux 提示及问题解析

```
[root@ygx100 RPMS]# rpm -ivh bash-2.05b-20.i386.rpm
warning: bash-2.05b-20.i386.rpm: V3 DSA signature: NOKEY, key ID db42a60e
Preparing...                ########################################### [100%]
        package bash-2.05b-20 is already installed
[root@ygx100 RPMS]#
```

Figure 5-1　Prompt map of rpm

具体问题见 Figure 5-1,解析：

rpm -ivh bash-2.05b-20.i386.rpm：用 rpm 命令安装 bash-2.05b-20.i386.rpm,并显示详细进度。

Preparing…：准备中。

Package bash-2.05b-20 is already installed：bash-2.05b-20 包已经安装过。

```
[root@localhost 桌面]# ping -c 1 192.168.95.1
PING 192.168.95.1 (192.168.95.1) 56(84) bytes of data.
64 bytes from 192.168.95.1: icmp_seq=1 ttl=128 time=1.92 ms
--- 192.168.95.1 ping statistics ---
1 packets transmitted, 1 received, 0% packet loss, time 2ms
rtt min/avg/max/mdev = 1.920/1.920/1.920/0.000
```

解析如下。

这是本机和 192.168.95.1 这个 IP 能连通所得到的回复。

第一行中的[root@localhost 桌面]表示 localhost 这台主机上的名为 root 的超级用户所进行或用该权限所做的操作,当前文件夹是桌面。"♯"这个符号是代表 root 超级用户权限下的命令提示符。ping -c 1 192.168.95.1,其中的-c count 就是发送 count 次 ECHO_REQUEST(回传请求)数据包,这里是-c 1 意味着发送一次 ECHO_REQUEST(回传请求)数据包。

第二行中,ping 命令用 56(84) bytes of data 包数据去测试 192.168.95.1 这个 IP 地址。

第三行中收到从192.168.95.1这个IP返回来的64字节数据包,用时1.92 ms,icmp_seq为1,ttl字段是128,TTL字段指定IP数据包被路由器丢弃之前运行通过的最大网段数量。最大值设置为128(最大可以设置为255),是为了防止数据包在网络中无限循环,而限定的最大转发次数,每经过一个路由器该字段就会减1,如果减到0还没到达目的主机,则会自动丢弃,并返回request time out(请求超时)。

第四行中是一个提示,提示这是"---192.168.95.1 ping 统计信息---",就是关于192.168.95.1这个IP地址的ping命令的统计信息。

第五行中说明具体情况,发送1个数据包,接收1个数据包,0%的数据包丢失,时间为2 ms。

六行分别说明了rtt的最小/平均/最大/ mdev 值=1.920 / 1.920 / 1.920 / 0.000。

这个命令回复中没有出现timeout字样,timeout代表超时,没有出现则代表没有超时,说明网络是连通的。

```
[root@localhost 桌面]# ping -c 1 192.168.95.1
PING 192.168.95.1 (192.168.95.1) 56(84) bytes of data.
--- 192.168.95.1 ping statistics ---
1 packets transmitted, 0 received, 100% packet loss, time 10001
```

解析如下。

这是本机和192.168.95.1这个IP不能连通所得到的其中一种回复。不能连通,除了网线问题,还有主机关机等各种问题。

前面三行和上面一样,最后一行不一样:已发送1个数据包,接收0个数据包,100%的数据包丢失,时间10001,这就说明网络不通或对方主机关闭,总之没办法成功通信。

```
[root@localhost 桌面]# pin -c 1 192.168.95.1
bash: pin: command not found
```

解析如下。

第二行意义为:在shell中的bash版本中找不到pin这个命令,意思就是这个命令拼错了,我们如果仔细点,可以发现pin少了个字母g,应该是ping才对。

具体问题见Figure 5-2,解析如下。

This file was automatically generated by the /lib/udev/write_net_rules program. run by the persistent-net-generaror. rules rules file:该文件由/ lib / udev / write_net_rules 程序自动生成,由persistent-net-generaror. rules 规则文件运行。

You can modify it,as long as you keep each rule on a single:您可以修改它,只要将每个规则都放在一个整体里。

PCI devices 0x1022:0x2000(pcnet32),PCI 设备 0x1022:0x2000(pcnet32)。

ACTION=="add":操作参数为"增加"。

ATTR{address}=="00:0c:29:79:ac:85",即网卡地址为00:0c:29:79:ac:85。

NAME=="eth0":名称是eth0。

"etc/udev/rules. d/70-persistent-net. rules"11L,589C:位于etc目录下的udev目录下的rules. d目录下的70-persistent-net. rules文件共有11行,589个字符。

Figure 5-2　NIC drift

Figure 5-3　Network restart

具体问题见 Figure 5-3,解析如下。

service network restart：重启网络服务。

Figure 5-4　IP tables stop and status

具体问题见 Figure 5-4,解析如下。

Service iptables stop：防火墙服务关闭。

Service iptables status：查询防火墙服务状态。

具体问题见 Figure 5-5,解析如下。

DEVICE＝eth0：设备名称。

TYPE＝Ethernet：接口对应的网络类型,这里是以太网。

BOOTPROTO＝none：表示如何获得 IP,有三个参数可以供选择,static 手动指定 IP,dhcp 使用 DHCP 获得 IP,none 表示启动时不使用任何协议。

HWADDR＝00:0c:29:16:24:86 表示使用的 MAC 地址,可以不使用。

ONBOOT＝yes：开机是否开启这个接口,有 yes 或 no 两个选择。

NETMASK＝255.255.255.0：子网掩码。

```
DEVICE=eth0
TYPE=Ethernet
UUID=786ffa25-97e7-4958-b04f-a2f28ccdddb5
ONBOOT=no
NM_CONTROLLED=yes
BOOTPROTO=none
IPADDR=192.168.233.200
NETMASK=255.255.255.0
IPV6INIT=no
USERCTL=no
HWADDR=00:0C:29:16:24:86
PREFIX=24
DEFROUTE=yes
IPV4_FAILURE_FATAL=yes
NAME="System eth0"
LAST_CONNECT=1442224514
~
~
~
~
~
"/etc/sysconfig/network-scripts/ifcfg-eth0"  16L, 293C
```

Figure 5-5　IP Setup

IPADDR=192.168.233.200，IP 地址。

UDDI：全局唯一标识符，在系统中起作用。

NM_CONTROLLED：network manager 参数，立即生效。

DNS1：第一台 dns 服务器的地址。

DNS2：第二台 dns 服务器的地址。

USERCTL=no：设置为 no，只允许 root 用户控制该设备。

IPV6INIT：是否使用 IPv6。

NAME：定义设备名称。

LAST_CONNECT：上一连接。

DEFROUTE=yes：设置这个接口为默认路由。

PREFIX：前缀，子网掩码有几位。

上面的所有字段名都是大写。

Could not determine the server's fully qualified domain name, using 127.0.0.1 for ServerName.

解析如下。

无法确定服务器的标准域名，对域名服务器使用 127.0.0.1。

具体问题见 figure 5-6，解析如下。

这是用 ifconfig 命令测试所有网卡的基本所有设置，显示当前系统有效（活动）的网络接口信息。

```
[root@localhost 桌面]# ifconfig -a
eth0      Link encap:Ethernet  HWaddr 00:0C:29:55:36:17
          inet addr:192.168.59.200  Bcast:192.168.59.255  Mask:255.255.255.0
          inet6 addr: fe80::20c:29ff:fe55:3617/64 Scope:Link
          UP BROADCAST RUNNING MULTICAST  MTU:1500  Metric:1
          RX packets:49 errors:0 dropped:0 overruns:0 frame:0
          TX packets:29 errors:0 dropped:0 overruns:0 carrier:0
          collisions:0 txqueuelen:1000
          RX bytes:5446 (5.3 KiB)  TX bytes:2708 (2.6 KiB)
          Interrupt:19 Base address:0x2000

lo        Link encap:Local Loopback
          inet addr:127.0.0.1  Mask:255.0.0.0
          inet6 addr: ::1/128 Scope:Host
          UP LOOPBACK RUNNING  MTU:16436  Metric:1
          RX packets:24 errors:0 dropped:0 overruns:0 frame:0
          TX packets:24 errors:0 dropped:0 overruns:0 carrier:0
          collisions:0 txqueuelen:0
          RX bytes:1616 (1.5 KiB)  TX bytes:1616 (1.5 KiB)

[root@localhost 桌面]#
```

Figure 5-6　ifconfig

eth0：第一块以太网卡的名称，是网络卡的代号。

HWaddr：网络卡的硬件地址，俗称的 MAC 地址，本网卡的全球唯一编号为 00：0C：29：55：36：17。

inet addr：IPv4 的 IP 地址，就是这个网卡的 IP 地址，为 192.168.59.200。后续的 Bcast 代表的是 Broadcast 广播地址，为 192.168.59.155，Mask 代表 netmask 子网掩码，为 255.255.255.0。

inet6 addr：是 IPv6 版本的 IP，这里是 fe80::20c:29ff:fe55:3617/64。

MTU：最大传输单元(maximum transmission unit)是指一种通信协议的某一层上面所能通过的最大数据包大小(以字节为单位)。我们在使用互联网时进行的各种网络操作，都是通过一个又一个的"数据包"传输来实现的。而 MTU 指定了网络中可传输数据包的最大尺寸，在我们常用的以太网中，MTU 是 1 500 字节。超过此大小的数据包就会将多余的部分拆分再单独传输。

Metric：路由开销，是路由算法用以确定到达目的地的最佳路径的计量标准，如路径长度，这里是本地网卡，当然为 0。

RX：那一行代表的是网络由启动到目前为止的封包接收情况，packets 代表封包数，errors 代表封包发生错误的数量、dropped 代表封包由于有问题而遭丢弃的数量，等等。

TX：与 RX 相反，为网络由启动到目前为止的传送情况。

collisions：代表封包碰撞的情况，如果发生太多次，表示网络状况不太好，这里是 0，表示非常好。

txqueuelen：代表用来传输数据的缓冲区的储存长度。

RX bytes，TX bytes：总接收、发送字节总量分别为 5 446 和 2 708 字节。

lo 是系统的"环回"网络接口，是 loopback，是一个虚拟的网络接口，其 IP 地址永远是 127.0.0.1，通常用于对本机网络的测试。

具体问题见 Figure 5-7，解析如下。

从上到下分别为：用 ftp 命令访问 192.168.59.200，连接到 192.168.59.200 的 IP 上，编号 220，用户名为匿名用户——anonymous，输入密码(这里密码输入后不会出现 * 号，直

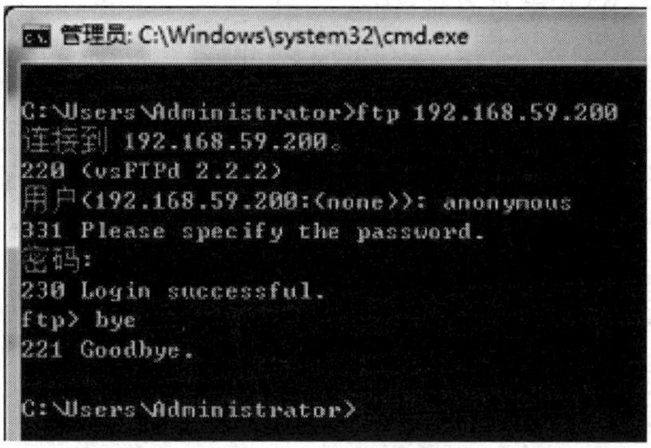

第 5 章 其他专业英语

Figure 5-7 Username and password

接回车就好），然后编号 230，登录成功，这时输入命令 bye，要求退出 ftp 访问，计算机回复编号 221，"再见"，这时候就直接断开 ftp 访问了。

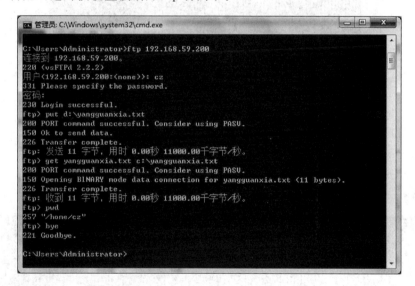

Figure 5-8 Upload and download

Figure 5-8 的解析如下。

ftp　192.168.59.200：用 ftp 访问 192.168.59.200。

用户名为 cz，直接输入后回车就可以。

331　Please specify the password：请指定密码，

然后输入密码后回车。

230　Login successful：登录成功。

Put　d:\yangguanxia.txt，即上传本机 d 盘上的 yangguanxia.txt，是同名上传到默认位置。

200　PORT command successful：编号 200，端口命令成功执行。

Consider using　PASV：正在考虑使用 PASV。

150　Ok to send data：编号 150，可以发送数据。

117

226　Transfer complete：编号 226，传输完成。

get yangguanxia.txt c：\yangguanxia.txt，即下载 ftp 服务器中的默认位置的 yangguanxia.txt 文件到本地主机的 C 盘，名字也为 yangguanxia.txt。

200　PORT command successful. Consider using　PASV：编号 220，端口命令成功，正在考虑使用 PASV。

150　Openning BINARY mode data connection for yangguanxia.txt ＜11bytes＞：编号 150，打开 yangguangxia.txt 的二进制数据连接，传输 11 个字节的数据。

226　Transfer complete：编号 226，传输完成。

pwd：查询服务器中当前路径为/home/cz 的目录。

bye：申请切断。

Goodbye：服务器接受切断，服务断开。

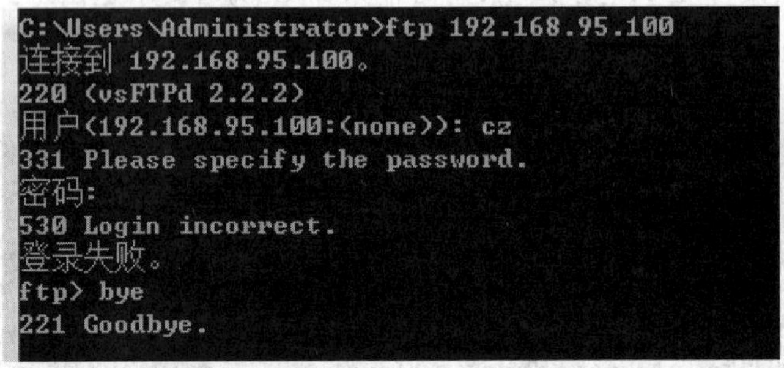

Figure 5-9　Login incorrect

Figure 5-9 解析如下。

Login incorrect：登录失败。

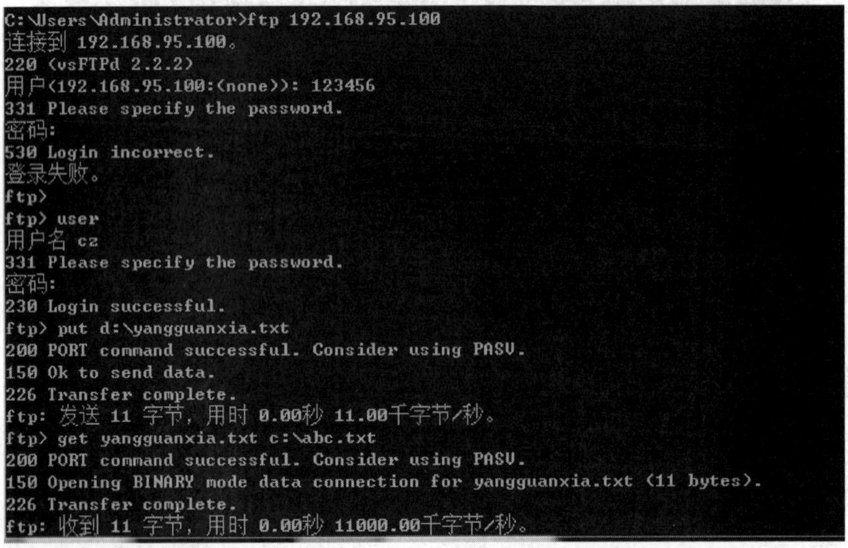

Figure 5-10　Reminder of ftp

Figure 9-10 是 ftp 提示。

5.2 虚拟机英文提示及解决方法

Figure 5-11　Network

Figure 5-11 的解析如下。

VMware Network Adater VMnet1：名为 VMnet1 的虚拟机网卡。

Figure 5-12 解析如下。

Hardware：硬件。

Options：选件。

Device：设备。

Summary：摘要。

Memory 1 024 MB：内存 1 024 兆字节。

Processors 1：处理器 1 个。

Hard Disk(IDE) 8 GB：硬盘 8 个 G 字节。

CD/DVD(IDE)　Using file D:\软件\rhel-serve…，即 CD／DVD(IDE)使用文件 D:\软件\ rhel-serve…。

Floppy　Auto detect：自动检测软盘。

Network Adapter　Host-only：网络适配器仅主机。

USB controller　Present：USB 控制器存在。

Sound Card　Auto detect：声卡自动检测。

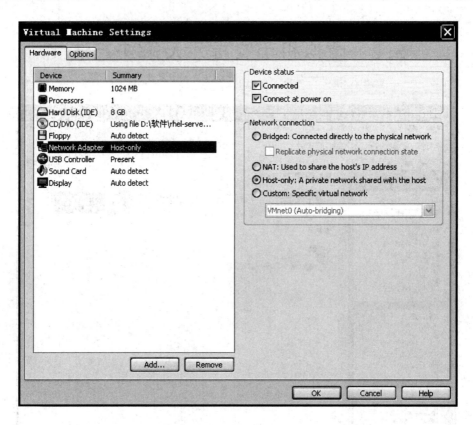

Figure 5-12　Hardware setup

Display　Auto detect:显示器自动检测。

Add:加。

Remove:移除。

Device status:设备状态。

Connected:已连接。

Connected at power on:通电时自动连接。

Network connection:网络连接。

Bridged:桥接。

Host-only:仅主机。

Custom:自定义。

Connected directly to the physical network:直接连接到物理网络。

Used to share the host's IP address:用于共享主机的 IP 地址。

A private network shared with the host:与主机共享的专用网络。

Specific virtual network:特定的虚拟网络。

OK:确定。

Cancel:取消。

Help:帮助。

安装软件的时候经常会看见上面的英文,Figure 5-13 的解析如下。

Modify,repair,or remove the program:修改,修复和删除程序。

Select new program features to add or select currently installed features to remove:选择要添加的新程序功能或选择要删除的当前安装功能。

Reinstall all program features installed by the provious setup:重新安装以前的安装程序安装的所有程序功能。

Remove all installed features:删除所有已安装的功能。

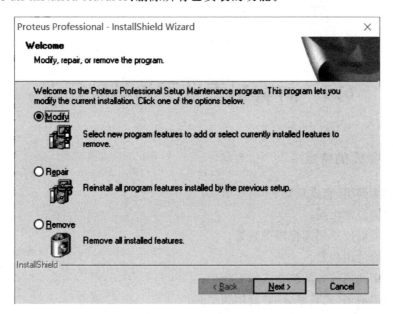

Figure 5-13　Modify and repair and remove

第6章 计算机专业英语

6.1 计算机专业英语基础知识

6.1.1 用词的特点

（1）名词性词组、合成新词、介词短语多；
（2）缩略词经常出现；
（3）单个动词比动词词组用得频繁；
（4）缩略语使用频繁；
（5）常使用动词或名词演化成的形容词；
（6）非限定动词（尤其是分词）使用频率高；
（7）半技术词汇多；
（8）希腊词根和拉丁词根比例大。

例：This approach mitigates complexity separating the concerns of the front end, which typically revolve around language semantics, error checking, and the like, from the concerns of the back end, which concentrates on producing output that is both efficient and correct.

词汇：
mitigate	使减轻；使缓和
separate from	分离；把……和……分开
concerns of	……的忧虑；……关切的事
revolve around	围绕……转动；以……为中心
semantics	语义[计算机科学技术]

译文：这种方法降低了把处理语义、检测错误等前端工作和主要产生正确有效输出的后端工作分离开来的复杂性。

6.1.2 语法的特点

科学技术关注于客观的普遍规律和对过程、概念的描述，其客观性和无人称性需要通过语法结构来反映。

（1）长句多；

(2) 专业术语多；

(3) 被动语态使用频繁；

(4) 常用 It… 句型结构；

(5) 在说明书、手册中广泛使用祈使语句；

(6) 用虚拟语气表达假设或建议。

1. 在说明事理并涉及各种前提和条件时，可以用虚拟语气。

例：Were there no plants, there would be no photosynthesis and life could not go on.

译文：如果没有植物，就没有光合作用，生命就无法继续下去。

2. 祈使语句常用来表示指示、建议、劝告和命令等意思，可以用于说明书、操作规程和注意事项等资料中。

例 1：Insert new diskette for drive A and strike any key when ready.

译文：将新盘插入 A 驱动器，准备好后按任一键。

例 2：Must be structure field name.

译文：需要的是结构字段名，但得到的是其他内容。

6.1.3　句型结构

(1) It is ＋名词＋从句

It is a fact that…

It is a question that…　……是个问题

It is no wonder that…　毫无疑问……

It is the law of nature that…　……是自然规律

It is a common practice to…　通常的做法是……

(2) It is ＋形容词＋从句

It is necessary that…　有必要……

It is clear that…　很清楚……

It is important that…　重要的是……

It is natural that…　很自然的是……

(3) It is ＋过去分词＋从句

It is said that…　据说……

It is believed that…　确信……

It has been proved that…　已证明……

It is generally considered that…　人们普遍认为……

(4) It is ＋介词短语＋从句

It is from this point of view that…　由此看来……

It is of great significance that…　……具有重大的意义

It is only under these conditions that…　只有在这些条件下才能……

(5) It is ＋不及物动词＋从句

It follows that…　由此可见……

It turned out that…　结果是……

It may be that…　　可能……

It stands to reason that…　　显然……

例： It was in the 1940's that the first computer was built.

译文： 第一台数字计算机建成于 20 世纪 40 年代。

例： It is necessary to learn Visual Basic.

译文： 学习 Visual Basic 是很有必要的。

6.1.4　词汇类型

(1) 技术词汇

技术词汇(technical words)的意义狭窄、单一，一般只使用在各自的专业范围内，因而专业性很强。这类词一般较长并且越长词义越狭窄，出现的频率也不高。

例如：bandwidth(带宽)、flip-flop(触发器)、superconductivity(超导性)、hexadecimal(十六进制)、amplifier(放大器)等。

(2) 次技术词汇

次技术词汇(sub-technical words)是指词义不受上下文限制，各专业中出现频率都很高的词。这类词往往在不同的专业中具有不同的含义。

例如：register 在计算机系统中表示寄存器，在电学中表示计数器、记录器，在乐器中表示音区，而在日常生活中则表示登记簿、名册、挂号信等。

(3) 特用词

在日常英语中，为使语言生动活泼，常使用一些短小的词或词组。而在专业英语中，表达同样的意义时，为了准确、正式、严谨，不引起歧义却往往选用一些较长的特用词(big words)。这些词在非专业英语中极少使用但却属于非专业英语。

(4) 功能词

功能词(function words)包括介词、连词、冠词、代词等。研究表明，在专业英语中，出现频率最高的 10 个词都是功能词，其顺序为 the、of、in、and、to、is、that、for、are、be。下例中 14 个词中功能词就占了 6 个。

例： When the record is operated in the record mode, previous recordings are automatically erased.

译文： 当录音机工作在录音模式时，以前的录音被自动擦除。

6.1.5　词汇来源

(1) 来源于英语中的普通词，但被赋予了新的词义

例： Work is the transfer of energy expressed as the product of a force and the distance through which its point of application moves in the direction of the force.

本句中的 "work、energy、product、force" 都是从普通词汇中借来的物理学术语。"work" 的意思不是 "工作"，而是 "功"；"energy" 的意思不是 "活力"，而是 "能"；"product" 的意思不是 "产品"，而是 "乘积"；"force" 的意思不是 "力量"，而是 "力"。

译文： 功是能的传递，表达为力与力的作用点沿着力的方向移动的距离的乘积。

(2) 来源于希腊语或拉丁语

例：thermo　　　　热（希腊语）
　　thesis　　　　论文（希腊语）
　　parameter　　参数（拉丁语）
　　radius　　　　半径（拉丁语）
　　formula　　　公式（拉丁语）
　　data　　　　　数据（拉丁语）

(3) 由两个或两个以上的单词组成合成词

合成词是专业英语中另一大类词汇，其组成面广，多数以连字符"-"连接单词构成，或者采用短语构成。合成方法有名词＋名词、形容词＋名词、动词＋副词、名词＋动词、介词＋名词、形容词＋动词等。

例：file ＋ based → file-based　　基于文件的
　　Windows ＋ based → Windows-based　以 Windows 为基础的
　　object ＋ oriented → object-oriented　面向对象的
　　thread ＋ oriented → thread-oriented　面向线程的
　　point ＋ to ＋ point → point-to-point　点到点
　　plug ＋ and ＋ play → plug-and-play　即插即用
　　in ＋ put → input　　输入
　　out ＋ put → output　输出
　　feed ＋ back → feedback　反馈
　　fan ＋ in → fanin　　扇入
　　fan ＋ out → fanout　扇出
　　on ＋ line → online　在线
　　in ＋ put → input　　输入
　　out ＋ put → output　输出
　　feed ＋ back → feedback　反馈
　　fan ＋ in → fanin　　扇入
　　fan ＋ out → fanout　扇出
　　on ＋ line → online　在线

由两个或更多词组成的专业术语，它的构成成分虽然看起来是独立的，但实际上是完整的概念。

例：liquid crystal　　　　液晶
　　computer language　　计算机语言
　　machine building　　　机器制造
　　linear measure　　　　长度单位
　　civil engineering　　　土木工程

(4) 派生词

派生也叫缀合。派生而来的专业词汇非常多，专业英语词汇大部分都是用派生法构成的，它是根据已有的词，通过对词根加上各种前缀和后缀构成的新词。这些词缀有名词词缀,如 inter-、sub-、in-、tele-、micro-等;有形容词词缀,如 im-、un-、-able、-al、-ing、-ed 等;有动词词缀,如 re-、under-、de-、-en、con-等。

例:multimedia   多媒体
　　multiprocessor   多处理器
　　interface   接口
　　Internet   互联网
　　microprocessor   微处理器
　　microcode   微代码
　　hypertext   超文本
　　hypermedia   超媒体
　　anti-   表示"反对"
　　counter-   表示"反对,相反"
　　contra-   表示"反对,相反"
　　de-   表示"减少,降低,否定"
　　dis-   表示"否定,除去"
　　in-   (i 在字母 n、l 前)表示"不"
　　im-   (i 在字母 m、b、p 前)表示"不"
　　mis-   表示"错误"
　　non-   表示"不,非"
　　un-   表示"不、未、丧失"
　　electric(形容词)＋ity → electricity(名词:电,电学)
　　liquid(名词)＋ize → liquidize(动词:液化)
　　conduct(动词)＋or → conductor(名词:导体)
　　invent(动词)＋ion → invention(名词:发明)
　　propel(动词)＋l＋er → propeller(名词:推进器)
　　simple(形容词)＋icity → simplicity(名词:单纯,注意拼写有变化)
　　maintain(动词)＋ance → maintenance(名词:维修,注意拼写有变化)

(5) 借用词

借用词是指借用公共英语及日常生活用语中的词汇来表达专业含义。借用词一般来自厂商名、商标名、产品代号名、发明者名、地名等,也可通过将公共英语词汇演变成专业词意而实现。

例:cache   高速缓存
　　semaphore   信号量
　　firewall   防火墙
　　mail bomb   邮件炸弹
　　fitfall   子程序入口
　　flag   标志,状态

(6) 通过词性转化构成新词

通过词性转化构成新词指一个词不变化词形,而由一种词性转化为另一种或几种词性,有时发生重音或尾音的变化。

英语中名词、形容词、副词、介词可以转化成动词,动词、形容词、副词、介词可以转化成名词。但最活跃的是名词转化成动词和动词转化成名词。

例:coordinate(动词)协调 → coordinate(名词)坐标
　　center(名词)中心 → center(动词)集中
　　Asian(名词)亚洲人 → Asian(形容词)亚洲的
　　break(动词)打破 → break(名词)间歇
　　close(关上) → close(副词)靠近
　　clear(形容词)明确的 → clear(动词)清除

(7) 省略词

词汇缩略是指将较长的单词取其首部或主干构成与原词同义的短单词,或者将组成词汇短语的各个单词的首字母拼接为一个大写字母的字符串。

通常词汇缩略在文章索引、前序、摘要、文摘、电报、说明书、商标等中频繁采用。

对计算机专业来说,在程序语句、程序注释、软件文档、互联网信息、文件描述中也采用了大量的缩略词作为标识符、名称等。

例:maths——mathematics 数学
　　ad——advertisement 广告
　　kilo——kilogram 公斤
　　dir——directory 目录
　　lab——laboratory 实验室
　　radar——radio detection and ranging 雷达
　　transceiver——transistor receiver 收发机
　　telesat——telecommunications satellite 通信卫星

首字词与缩略词基本相同,区别在于首字词必须逐字母念出。

例:CAD——computer aided design(计算机辅助设计)
　　CPU——central process unit(中央处理器)
　　DBMS——data base management system(数据库管理系统)
　　UFO——unidentified flying object(不明飞行物)
　　CGA——color graphics adapter(彩色图形适配器)

缩略词不一定由某个词的首字母组成,有些缩略词仅由一个单词变化而来。

例:e.g.——for example
　　Ltd.——limited
　　sq.——square
　　ROM——read only memory(只读存储器)
　　RAM——random access memory(随机访问存储器)
　　RISC——reduced instruction set computer(精简指令集计算机)
　　CISC——complex instruction set computer(复杂指令集计算机)
　　COBOL——common business oriented language(面向商务的通用语言)

6.1.6 计算机专用术语与命令

(1) 专用的软件名称及计算机厂商名

Authorware　专业多媒体软件(属于 Macromedia 公司)
Dreamweaver　网页设计软件(属于 Macromedia 公司)
MATLAB　科学计算软件(属于 Math Works 公司)
著名计算机公司译名如下：

Microsoft　微软　　　　　　　　Philip　飞利浦
DELL　戴尔　　　　　　　　　　Samsung　三星
Panasonic 松下　　　　　　　　 ASUS　华硕

(2) DOS 系统

DOS(disk operating system)是个人计算机磁盘操作系统,DOS 是一组非常重要的程序,它帮助用户建立、管理程序和数据,也管理计算机系统的设备。

DOS 是一种层次结构,包括 DOS BIOS(基本输入输出系统)、DOS 核心部分和 DOS COMMAND(命令处理程序)。

(3) 计算机专用命令和指令

大部分的计算机语言的词汇都取自英语词汇中一个很小的子集和最常用的数学符号。由于各个计算机指令系统所具有的功能大致相同,各个程序设计语言也大体包含了函数、过程、子程序、条件、循环以及输入和输出等部分。系统命令与程序无关,而且语法结构简单。每一个处理器都具有很多指令,每一台机器也具有很多系统命令,不同的操作系统也定义了不同的操作命令。

① 创建目录 MD(make directory)

② 改变目录 CD(change directory)

③ 重命名 REN(rename)

④ 中断请求 INT(call to interrupt procedure)

6.1.7 网络专用术语

(1) Internet 专用缩写术语

① TCP/IP 协议:Internet 使用的一组网络协议,其中 IP 是 Internet Protocol,即网际协议;TCP 是 Transmission Control Protocol,即传输控制协议。IP 协议提供基本的通信,TCP 协议提供应用程序所需要的其他功能。

② SMTP:Simple Mail Transfer Protocol,简单邮件传送协议,用于电子邮件传送。

③ HTTP:Hypertext Transfer Protocol,超文本传送协议,用于 World Wide Web 服务。

④ SNMP:Simple Network Management Protocol,简单网络管理协议,用于网络管理。

(2) Internet 服务

① E-mail:电子邮件,指通过计算机网络收发信息的服务。电子邮件是 Internet 上最普遍的应用,它加强了人与人之间沟通。

② Telnet：远程登录。用户可以通过专门的 Telnet 命令登录到一个远程计算机系统，该系统根据用户账号判断用户对本系统的使用权限。

③ FTP：File Transfer Protocol，文件传输协议。利用 FTP 协议可以直接将远程系统上任何类型的文件下载到本地计算机上，或将本地文件上传到远程系统。它是实现 Internet 上软件共享的基本方式。

（3）Internet 地址

① Domain Name。域名，它是 Internet 中主机地址的一种表示方式。域名采用层次结构，每一层构成一个子域名，子域名之间用点号隔开并且从右到左逐渐具体化。域名的一般表示形式为：计算机名、网络名、机构名、一级域名。

② 电子邮件地址。在 Internet 上，电子邮件（E-mail）地址具有如下统一的标准格式：用户名@主机域名。例如，wang@online.sh.cn 是一个电子邮件的地址。

6.2　计算机专业英语阅读

6.2.1　计算机的历史

The history of the computer

The first large-scale electronic computer was the Electronic Numerical Integrator and Computer (ENIAC), which became operational in 1946. From that start, computer has developed through four so-called generations, or stages, each one characterized by smaller size, and less expense than its predecessor.

(1) First Generation (1944 – 1958)

In the earliest general-purpose computer, most input and output media were punched cards and magnetic tape. Main memory was almost exclusively made up of hundreds of vacuum tubes—although one computer used a magnetic drum for main memory. These computers were somewhat unreliable because the vacuum tubes failed frequently. They were also slower than any microcomputer used today, produced a tremendous amount of heat, and were very large. They could run only one program at a time.

(2) Second Generation (1959 – 1963)

By the early 1960s, transistors and some other solid-state devices that were much smaller than vacuum tubes were being used for much of the computer. Magnetic cores, which looked like very small metal washers strung together by wires that carried electricity, became the most widely used type of main memory. Removable magnetic disk packs, stacks of disks connected by a common spindle, were introduced as storage devices. Second-generation machines tended to be smaller, more reliable, and significantly faster than first-generation.

(3) Third Generation (1964 – 1970)

In the third period, the integrated circuit (IC) — a complete electronic circuit that packages transistors and other electronic components on a small silicon chip — replaced traditional transistorized circuitry. Integrated circuits are cost-effective because individual components don't need to be wired directly to the computer's system board. The use of magnetic disks for secondary data storage became widespread, and computers began to support such capabilities as multiprogramming (processing several programs simultaneously) and timesharing (people using the same computer simultaneously). Mini computers were being widely used by the early 1970s and were taking some of the business away from the established mainframe market. Processing that formerly required the processing power of a mainframe could now be done on a minicomputer.

(4) Fourth Generation (1971 – Now)

Large-scale integrated (LSI) and very-large-scale integrated (VLSI) circuits were developed that contained hundreds to millions of transistors on a tiny chip. In 1971, Ted Hoff of Intel developed the microprocessor, which packaged an entire CPU, complete with memory, logic, and control circuits, on a single chip. The microprocessor and VLSI circuit technology caused radical changes in computers — in their size, appearance, cost, availability and capability, and they started the process of miniaturization — the development of smaller and smaller computers. Also during this time, computer's main memory capacity increased, and its cost decreased, which directly affected the types and usefulness of software that could be used. Software applications like word processing, electronic spreadsheets, database management programs, painting and drawing programs, desktop publishing, and so forth became commercially available, giving more people reasons to use a computer.

6.2.2 计算机如何工作

How Does a Computer Work

Let us use the system shown in figure 6-1 to show you how a typical computer works. A computer is controlled by a stored program, so if we want to use a computer, the first step is copying the program from diskette into memory. Now the processor can begin executing instructions; the data input from the keyboard are stored in memory. The processor processes the data and then stores the results back into memory. At last, we can get the result.

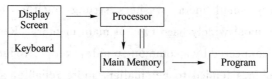

Figure 6-1　Computer system

Now we can see that a computer system consists of four basic components. An input device provides data. The data are stored in memory, which also holds a program. Under the controls of the program, the computer's processor processes the data. The results flow from the computer to an output device. Let us introduce the system components one by one, beginning with the processor.

The processor, usually called the central processing unit (CPU) or main processor, is the heart of a computer. It is the CPU that in fact processes or manipulates data and controls all the rest parts of the computer. How can it manage its job? The secret is software. Without a program to provide control, a CPU can do nothing. How can a program guide the CPU through the processes? Let us consider from the basic element of a program—instruction.

An instruction is composed of two parts: an operation code and one or more operands (figure 6-2). The operation codes tell the CPU what to do and the operands tell the CPU where to find the data to be manipulated.

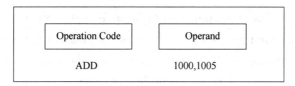

Figure 6-2　Instruction

The processor contains four major components (figure 6-3): a clock, an instruction control, an arithmetic and logic unit (usually shortened ALU) and several registers. The clock generates precisely timed pulses of current that synchronize the processor's other components. Then the instruction control unit determines the location of the next instruction to be executed and fetches it from the main memory. The arithmetic and logic unit performs arithmetic operations (such as addition and subtraction) and logic operations (such as testing a value to see if it is true or false), while the registers are temporary storage devices that hold control information, key data and some intermediate results. Since the registers are located in the CPU (figure 6-4), the processing speed is faster than the main memory. Then which is the key component to a computer's speed? It is the clock! In more detail, it is the clock's frequency that decides a computer's processing speed. When we buy a computer, we usually consider the main frequency first, and that means a clock's frequency.

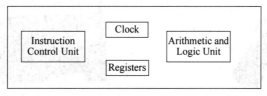

Figure 6-3　Processor's four major components

Transistors are the basic building blocks of microprocessors. A single microchip may contain millions of transistors. When electric current is allowed to pass through, the switch is on. This represents 1 bit. If the current does not pass through, the switch is off. This represents 0 bit. Different combinations of transistors represent different combinations of bits, which are used to represent special characters, letters, and digits.

Figure 6-4　CPU

We often hear of input/output system (or I/O), What's the I/O system? In computing, I/O is the communication between an information processing system (such as a computer) and the outside world. Inputs are the signals or data received by the system, and outputs are the signals or data sent from it. I/O devices are used by a person (or other system) to communicate with the computer. For example, The keyboard and the mouse (figure 6-5) may be an input devices for the computer, while monitors(figure 6-6) and printers are considered output devices. Modem (figure 6-7) and network interface cards (NIC figure 6-8) typically serve for both input and output devices.

Figure 6-5　Keyboard and mouse　　　　　Figure 6-6　Monitors

Figure 6-7　Modem　　　　　Figure 6-8　NIC

The mouse and the keyboard take as input physical devices. The user use them input the information, and the Input devices convert it into the signal that a computer can understand. The output information from these devices is input for the computer. Similarly, the printer and the monitor take as input signal that a computer output. They convert these signals into symbols that the user can see or read. These interactions between the computer and the user are called human-computer interaction. Memory is the devices that the CPU can read and write to directly, with individual instructions. In computer architecture, the combination of the CPU and the main memory is considered the brain of a computer. and from that point of view any transfer of information from or to that combination, for example to or from a disk drive, is considered I/O. The CPU and its supporting circuitry provide memory-mapped I/O that is used in low-level computer programming, such as the implementation of device drivers. An I/O algorithm is one designed to exploit locality and perform efficiently when data reside on secondary storage, such as a disk drive. A computer uses memory-mapped I/O accesses hardware by reading and writing to specific.

A computer uses memory-mapped I/O accesses hardware by reading and writing to specific memory locations, using the same assembly language instruction that computer would normally use to access memory.

6.2.3　关键词

hardware *n*. 硬件	mouse *n*. 鼠标	keyboard *n*. 键盘
scanner *n*. 扫描机	printer *n*. 打印机	circuit *n*. 电路
wire *n*. 导线	cable *n*. 电缆线	motherboard *n*. 主板
speaker *n*. 音箱	memory *n*. 内存	instruction *n*. 指令
headphone *n*. 耳机	command *n*. 命令	speaker *n*. 扬声器
audio *n*. 音频	projector *n*. 投影仪	scanner *n*. 扫描机
joystick *n*. 游戏杆	microphone *n*. 麦克风	peripheral *n*. 外围设备
output device 输出设备	input device 输入设备	display screen 显示器
light pen 光笔	auxiliary storage 辅助存储器	inner bus 内部总线
file folder 文件夹	facsimile machine 传真机	digital data 数字数据
data stream 数据流	pointing device 定点设备	camera 摄像头
digital camera 数码相机	graphic tablet 图形写字板	RAM 随机存取存储器
ROM 只读存储器		

参考文献

[1] 程钢.城市轨道交通专业英语(运营管理方向)[M].北京:电子工业出版社,2017.
[2] 黄星,黄汽驰.汽车英语[M].3版.北京:人民邮电出版社,2014.
[3] 韩美玲,赵辉.汽车实用英语[M].西安:西安交通大学出版社,2014.
[4] 赵巍巍.城市轨道交通专业英语[M].北京:人民交通出版社,2011.
[5] 陈宁,张艳丽.汽车专业英语[M].北京:北京邮电出版社,2013.
[6] 沈彬彬,吴志平.汽车专业英语[M].上海:上海交通大学,2016.
[7] 李俊玲,汽车工程专业英语[M].北京:机械工业出版社,2005.
[8] 黄小莉,夏凌,胡宏平.信息工程专业英语[M].西安:西安电子科技大学出版社,2015.
[9] 卜艳萍,周伟.计算机专业英语[M].北京:人民邮电出版社,2017.
[10] 朱龙,孙雅妮,谢宇.计算机专业英语[M].北京:人民邮电出版社,2012.
[11] 吕云翔.计算机专业英语[M].北京:人民邮电出版社,2016.

附录　ACM 词汇

abnormal distribution	非正态分布
acute angle	锐角
acute triangle	锐角三角形
add	v. 加
addend	n. 加数
additional	adj. 额外
adjacent	adj. 相邻
aggregate	n. 集合
albeit	conj. 尽管,即使
algebra	n. 代数
algorithm	n. 运算法则
alternately	adv. 轮流地
ambiguously	adv. 不明确地
amplitude	n. 振幅
anagram	n. 相同字母异序词,字谜
angle	n. 角
arbitrary	n. 算术
arc	n. 弧
arc sine	反正弦
arc cosine	反余弦
arc tangent	反正切
arc cotangent	反余切
arc secant	反正割
arc cosecant	反余割
area	n. 面积
arithmetic	n. 算术　adj. 算术的
array	n. 数组
ascending	adj. 升序
augend	n. 被加数
average	n. 平均数
axiom	n. 公理
axis	n. 轴
bar graph	条形统计图
barycentre	n. 重心

base	n. 底
binary system	二进制
binary code	二进制码
binary digit	二进制位,二进制数字
binary	adj. 二进制的 n. 二进制
bit	n. 比特,二进制的一位
bitwise	n. 按位
branch	n. 分支,支线
broken line graph	折线统计图
bulb	n. 灯泡
bump	n. & v. 碰撞,肿块,突起
byte	n. 字节
byte streams	字节数据流
calculate	v. 计算
calculation	n. 计算
calculus	n. 微积分
carry	n. 进位
case	n. 案例、用例
case sensitive	区分大小写
cell	n. 单元
centre	n. 圆心
channel	n. 通道,信道
character	n. 字符
check digit	校验数位
circle	n. 圆
circumcircle	n. 外切圆
circumference	n. 圆周
clockwise	adj. 顺时针方向的
coefficient	n. 系数
coefficients	n.(pl.) 系数
coffers	n. 保险柜
column	n. 列
combination	n. 组合
complement	n. 补集
complex number	复数
comma	n. 逗号
concave	adj. 凹的
cone	n. 圆锥
configuration	n. 配置,格局,形状
congruent	adj. 全等
connect	v. 连
consecutive	adj. 连续的

constant	n. 常量、常数
contains	v. 包含
context	n. 上下文,背景,环境
converting	n. 转换
convex	adj. 凸的
coordinate	n. 坐标(系)
coordinates	n. 坐标系
cosecant	n. 余割
cosine	n. 余弦
cotangent	n. 余切
count	n. &v. 计数
counter	n. 计数器
cube	n. 三次方,立方,立方体
cube root	n. 三次方根,立方根
cubic equation	三次方程
current	adj. 当前
curve diagram	曲线统计图
cycle	n. &v. 循环、周期
cylinder	n. 圆柱
data	n. 数据
data processing	数据处理
data set	数据集
decagon	n. 十边形
decidability	n. 可解码性
decimal	n. 小数 adj. 小数的
decimal notation	十进制表示法
decimal places	小数位
decimal point	小数点
decimal system	十进制
definite integral	定积分
definition	n. 定义
degree	n. 角度
delimited	v. 定界,分隔
delimiter	n. 定界符,分隔符
denominator	n. 分母
denote	v. 表示、指示
derivation	n. 求导
derivative	n. 导数
descending	n. 递减、降序
determinant	n. 行列式
diameter	n. 直径
diamond	n. 菱形

differential	*n.* 微分
digit	*n.* 数字
digital	*adj.* 数字的
digit and letter	数字和字母
distribution	*n.* 分布
dividend	*v.* 被除数
divisible	*v.* 整除
division	*n.* 除法
divisor	*n.* 除数
dodecagon	*n.* 十二边形
domain	*n.* 定义域
duodecimal	*n.* 十二进制 *adj.* 十二进制的
duplicate	*n.* &*v.* 重复
edge	*n.* 边
element	*n.* 元素
ellipse	*n.* 椭圆
eliminated	*v.* 被淘汰
encoding	*n.* 编码
encryption	*n.* 加密
enneagon	*n.* 九边形
equal or greater	大于等于
equal or lesser	小于等于
equal	*v.* 等于
equation	*n.* 等式,方程式
equilateral polygon	正多边形
equilateral triangle	等边三角形
equivalent	*v.* 等于 *adj.* 相等的,相同的
escentre	*n.* 旁心
Euclidean	*adj.* 欧几里德的
distance	*n.* 距离
even number	偶数
evolution	*n.* 开方
exceed	*v.* 超过
excentre	*n.* 外心
exclusive	*adj.* 仅仅的,排除其他
exponent	*n.* 指数,幂
factorial	*n.* 阶乘,阶乘积
Fibonacci	*n.* 斐波那契序列
format	*n.* 格式
formula	*n.* 公式
fraction	*n.* 分数
prism	*n.* 棱台

cone	*n.* 圆台
function	*n.* 函数
generate	*v.* 生成
GCD	*n.* 最大公约数
geometry	*n.* 几何
given	*adj.* 指定的,所述的,考虑到,鉴于　*n.* 假设事实
graph	*n.* 图表
greater than	大于
greatest common divisor	最大公约数
height	*n.* 高
hemisphere	*n.* 半球
hendecagon	*n.* 十一边形
heptagon	*n.* 七边形
hexadecimal system	十六进制
hexadecimal notation	十六进制表示法
hexagon	*n.* 六边形
hexahedron	*n.* 六面体
histogram	*n.* 柱形统计图
horizontal	*n.* 横轴
hyperbola	*n.* 双曲线
hypotenuse	*n.* 斜边
hypothesis	*n.* 假设
identical	*adj.* 完全相同的
image	*n.* 图象
imaginary number	虚数
in addition to	除了
incentre	*n.* 内心
inclusive	*adj.* 包含的　*adv.* 包括　*n.* 包容性
indefinite integral	不定积分
index	*n.* 索引、指数、下标
indicating	*v.* 说明、指示
inequation	*n.* 不等式
infinity	*n.* 无穷大
infinitesimal	*n.* 无穷小
input	*v.* & *n.* 输入
inscribed circle	内切圆
insignificant digit	无效数字
instructions	*n.* 操作指南,用法说明
integer	*n.* 整数
integral	*n.* 积分
intersect	*v.* 相交
intersection	*n.* 交集

inversion	*n.* 倒置，颠倒，倒转
irrational number	无理数
isosceles triangle	等腰三角形
isosceles trapezoid	等腰梯形
key	*n.* 键，关键码
leap years	*n.* 闰年
leg	*n.* 直角边
least common multiple	最小公倍数
length	*n.* 长
lesser than	小于
lexicographically	*adv.* 按照字典顺序地
limit	*n.* 极限
line	*n.* 线
locus	*n.* 轨迹
logarithm	*n.* 对数
lowercase	*adj.* 小写的
machine language	机器语言
mapping	*n. & v.* 映射
martian	*n.* 火星（人）
matrices	*n.* 矩阵
matrix	*n.* 矩阵
median	*n.* 中位数，中间
memory	*n.* 存储器
minimize	*v.* 最小化
minuend	*n.* 被减数
minus	*prep.* 减
modulo	*prep.* 以……为模
monomial	*n.* 单项式
monotonicity	*n.* 单调性
multiplicand	*n.* 被乘数
multiplication	*n.* 乘
multiplicator	*n.* 乘数
multiply	*v.* 乘
natural number	自然数
negative	*n.* 负数　*adj.* 负的
network	*n.* 网络，网
node	*n.* 节点
non-empty	*adj.* 非空的
non-negative	*adj.* 非负的
zero	*n.* 零
number	*n.* 数
numerator	*n.* 分子

numeric	*adj.* 数字的,数值的
numerical	*adj.* 数字的,数值的
obtuse angle	钝角
obtuse triangle	钝角三角形
octagon	*n.* 八边形
octal	*adj.* 八进制
octet	*n.* 八位位组,八位字节
odd integer	奇整数
odd number	奇数
omit	*vt.* 省略
omitted	*adj.* 省略的
operation	*n.* 运算
operator	*n.* 运算符,操作员
order	*n.* 顺序 *v.* 排序
ordinal numbers	序数
origin	*n.* 原点
orthocentre	*n.* 垂心
output	*n.* &*v.* 输出
palindrom numbers	回文数
path	*n.* 路径
parabola	*n.* 抛物线
parallel	*n.* &*v.* 平行 *adj.* 平行的
parallelepiped	*n.* 平行六面体
parallelogram	*n.* 平行四边形
parity	*n.* 奇偶性
parity property	奇偶性
pending	*adj.* 待定的,未定的,即将发生的
pentagon	*n.* 五边形
pentahedron	*n.* 五面体
percent	*n.* 百分比
percentage	*n.* 百分点
percentile	*n.* 百分位数
perigon	*n.* 周角
perimeter	*n.* 周长
period	*n.* 周期
periodicity	*n.* 周期性
permutation	*n.* 排列
phase	*n.* 相位
pi	*n.* 圆周率
pixels	*n.* 像素
plane	*n.* 面
plus	*prep.* 加

point	n. 点
polygon	n. 多边形
polyhedron	n. 多面体
polynomial	n. 多项式
pop	v. 弹出
positive number	正数
positive	n. 正数　adj. 正的
post	v. 发布信息
power	n. & v. 乘方
power of four	四次方
power of n	n 次方
power	v. 快速前进
prefix	n. 前置代号
prime	n. 素数(质数)
prime factors	质数因子(素数因子)
prime number	质数,素数
printer	n. 打印机
printout	v. 打印输出
prism	n. 棱柱
probability	n. 概率,然率
process	n. & v. 处理
product	n. & v. (乘)积
programmer	n. 程序设计师
proposition	n. 命题
proportion	n. 比例
proportional	n. 按比例　adj. 按比例的
prove	v. 证明
punctuation	n. 标点符号
push	v. 压入
pyramid	n. 棱锥
Pythagorean theorem	勾股定理
quadratic equation	二次方程
quadrilateral	n. 四边形
quartic equation	四次方程
quotient	n. 商
radial	n. 射线
radian	n. 弧度
radius	n. 半径
radiuses	n. 半径
random	n. 随机　adj. 随意的
range	n. 值域
ratio	n. 比率

rational number	有理数
real number	实数
real-valued	$n.$ 实值
rectangle	$n.$ 矩形
rectangular	$adj.$ 矩形的
reduce	$v.$ 减少
reforestation	$n.$ 重新造林
refresh	$v.$ 使恢复
region	$n.$ 地区
remainder	$n.$ 差
remaining	$n. \& v.$ 剩余
remove	$n.$ 去掉,清除
respectively	$adv.$ 分别
retrieve	$v.$ 取回,检索数据
rhombus	$n.$ 菱形
right angle	直角
right triangle	直角三角形
right trapezoid	直角梯形
ring	$n.$ 环
root of four	四次方根
root of n	n 次方根
standard deviation	标准差
rotation	$n.$ 旋转
round	$n. \& v.$ 四舍五入
round down	下舍入
round up	上舍入
row	$n.$ 行
sample input	输入举例
sample output	输出举例
scalene triangle	不等边三角形
scenarios	$n.$ 脚本,剧情梗概,场景,情景
schema	$n.$ 计划,图表
secant	$n.$ 正割
sector	$n.$ 扇形
segment	$n.$ 线段,分割
semicircle	$n.$ 半圆
sentinel	$n. \& v.$ 标记
separate	$adj.$ 分开的,分隔
separate line	单独一行
sequence	$n.$ 序列,顺序,一系列,一连串
sequential	$adj.$ 顺序的
serial	$adj.$ 串行的,连续的

series	n. 数列, 级数
shift	n. &v. 移位, 移数
side	n. 边
signal	n. 信号
significant digit	有效数字
similar	adj. 相似的
simple equation	一次方程
simulation	n. 模拟
simultaneous	adj. 同时
sine	n. 正弦
singular	n. 单数
solid	n. 固体
sorting	n. 排序
space	n. 空格, 空间
spamming	n. 大量发出垃圾邮件
specification	n. 详述, 描述
specify	vt. 具体说明, 详述
sphere	n. 球
square	n. 二次方, 平方, 正方形, 二次幂
square root	二次方根, 平方根
stack	n. 一堆, 一摞, 一叠
standard	n. 栈
deviation	n. 标准差
statistics	n. 统计
step	n. 步
stick	n. 柴枝
straight angle	平角
straight line	直线
string	n. 字符串
structure	n. 结构
sub-collection	n. 子集合
subprogram	n. 子程序
subroutine	n. 子程序
subset	n. 子集
subsequence	n. 子序列
substring	n. 子串
subtraction	n. 减法
subtrahend	n. 减数
successive elements	连续元素, 其后继元素(紧挨着的后一个)
sum	n. 和
summand	n. 被加数
surface area	表面积

switch	n. 开关
symbol	n. 符号
system	n. 系统
tabulator	n. tab 键
tag	n. 标签
tangent	n. 正切
tangent	adj. 相切的
tedious	n. 冗长的,啰嗦的
terminate	v. 终止
tetrahedron	n. 四面体
theorem	n. 定理
tie	n. 平局 v. 与……平手
tournament	n. 锦标赛,联赛
trailing zeros	尾随零
transformation	n. 转变,改革,转换
trapezoid	n. 梯形 adj. 梯形的
triangle	n. 三角形
trigonometry	n. 三角
truncate	v. 删减,缩短
undersurface	n. 底面
unique	adj. 独特,独一无二的
union	n. 并集
unknown	n. 未知数
uppercase	n. 大写字母 adj. 大写的
valid	adj. 有效的
variable	n. 变量
variance	n. 方差
vertex	n. 顶点
vertical line	竖轴
void	n. 空集
volume	n. 体积
weight	n. 权
weighted average	加权平均数
whitespace	n. 空格
width	n. 宽
axis	n. 坐标轴
x-coordinate	n. 横坐标
y-coordinate	n. 纵坐标